First World War
and Army of Occupation
War Diary
France, Belgium and Germany

36 DIVISION
107 Infantry Brigade
Royal Irish Rifles
2nd Battalion
1 November 1917 - 28 February 1918

WO95/2502/4

The Naval & Military Press Ltd
www.nmarchive.com
Published in association with The National Archives

Published by

The Naval & Military Press Ltd

Unit 10 Ridgewood Industrial Park,

Uckfield, East Sussex,

TN22 5QE England

Tel: +44 (0) 1825 749494

www.naval-military-press.com

www.nmarchive.com

This diary has been reprinted in facsimile from the original. Any imperfections are inevitably reproduced and the quality may fall short of modern type and cartographic standards.

© Crown Copyright
Images reproduced by permission of The National Archives, London, England, 2015.

Contents

Document type	Place/Title	Date From	Date To
Heading	WO95/2502/4		
Heading	36th Division 107th Infy Bde 2nd Bn Roy. Irish Rif. Feb 1918-Mar 1919 From 25 Division 74 Bde		
Heading	107th Brigade. 36th Division. 2nd Battalion The Royal Irish Rifles March 1918		
War Diary	Grand Seraucourt	01/03/1918	06/03/1918
War Diary	In Line	07/03/1918	14/03/1918
War Diary	Grand Seraucourt	15/03/1918	21/03/1918
War Diary	Le Hamel-Happencourt Road.	22/03/1918	22/03/1918
War Diary	Cugny	23/03/1918	24/03/1918
War Diary	Avricourt Ref. Map Amiens	25/03/1918	25/03/1918
War Diary	Guerbigny	26/03/1918	26/03/1918
War Diary	Erches	27/03/1918	28/03/1918
War Diary	Nr. Coullemelle	29/03/1918	29/03/1918
War Diary	Vallennes	30/03/1918	30/03/1918
War Diary	Saleux	31/03/1918	31/03/1918
Heading	107th Brigade. 36th Division. 2nd Battalion The Royal Irish Rifles April 1918		
War Diary	Maisnieres	01/04/1918	03/04/1918
War Diary	Proven	04/04/1918	04/04/1918
War Diary	B.20.c.6.6.	05/04/1918	06/04/1918
War Diary	Poelcapelle Left-Sub-Sector	07/04/1918	12/04/1918
War Diary	Battle Zone	13/04/1918	17/04/1918
War Diary	B.20.c.6.6.	18/04/1918	20/04/1918
War Diary	Foch Fme.	21/04/1918	23/04/1918
War Diary	West Of Steenbeek	24/04/1918	27/04/1918
War Diary	Wagner Camp.	28/04/1918	30/04/1918
War Diary	Canal Bank.	01/05/1918	06/05/1918
War Diary	In The Line	07/05/1918	11/05/1918
War Diary	Canal Bank East.	12/05/1918	17/05/1918
War Diary	A.23.d.50.50.	18/05/1918	18/05/1918
War Diary	Steenje Camp. A.23.d.50.50.	19/05/1918	29/05/1918
War Diary	Right Sub-Sector.	30/05/1918	05/06/1918
War Diary	Road-Camp	06/06/1918	13/06/1918
War Diary	Peterborough Camp.	14/06/1918	20/06/1918
War Diary	Tunnellers Camp.	21/06/1918	24/06/1918
War Diary	Cassel And Robrouck Area	25/06/1918	27/06/1918
War Diary	Tunnellers Camp.	28/06/1918	02/07/1918
War Diary	P.32.c.2.7.	03/07/1918	06/07/1918
War Diary	Support Line Fontaine Schaexken Houck	07/07/1918	15/07/1918
War Diary	Support Line Fontaine Houck Ermitage	16/07/1918	23/07/1918
War Diary	Front Line Bn. H.Q. At Kopje Farm X.5.a.55.20.	24/07/1918	24/07/1918
War Diary	Kopje Farm X.5.a.55.20.	25/07/1918	31/07/1918
War Diary	Wigwam Copse	01/08/1918	08/08/1918
War Diary	La Manche Copse	09/08/1918	16/08/1918
War Diary	Left Bde Front Line Sector	17/08/1918	21/08/1918
War Diary	Support Line Mancee Copse R.29.c.50.45.	22/08/1918	25/08/1918
War Diary	La Manche Copse	26/08/1918	26/08/1918
War Diary	P.32.b. Central	27/08/1918	31/08/1918
War Diary	S.11.d.	01/09/1918	03/09/1918

War Diary	T.8.c.	04/09/1918	05/09/1918
War Diary	T.6.c.6.5.	06/09/1918	07/09/1918
War Diary	T.6.c.6.5. And Neuve Eglise	08/09/1918	12/09/1918
War Diary	Support Line	12/09/1918	15/09/1918
War Diary	R.27.a.10.10.	16/09/1918	19/09/1918
War Diary	Q.13.b.4.9.	20/09/1918	20/09/1918
War Diary	Esquelbecq	21/09/1918	26/09/1918
War Diary	Tunnellers Camp	27/09/1918	27/09/1918
War Diary	P And "F" Camps	28/09/1918	28/09/1918
War Diary	I.10.c.	29/09/1918	29/09/1918
War Diary	Becelaere	30/09/1918	30/09/1918
War Diary	West Of Terhand	01/10/1918	01/10/1918
War Diary	Terhand	02/10/1918	04/10/1918
War Diary	Cackle Copse	05/10/1918	05/10/1918
War Diary	Reutel	06/10/1918	13/10/1918
War Diary	J.16.d.	14/10/1918	14/10/1918
War Diary	L.24.a.45.80.	15/10/1918	15/10/1918
War Diary	G.23.c.	16/10/1918	16/10/1918
War Diary	F.27.a.	17/10/1918	18/10/1918
War Diary	B.19.c.	19/10/1918	21/10/1918
War Diary	19c.10.	22/10/1918	22/10/1918
War Diary	I.17.d.	23/10/1918	23/10/1918
War Diary	B.24.a.	24/10/1918	25/10/1918
War Diary	I.29.a.	26/10/1918	26/10/1918
War Diary	B.19.c.	27/10/1918	27/10/1918
War Diary	N.35.a.	28/10/1918	31/10/1918
Miscellaneous	The Following Casualties amongst Officers Occurred During The Month	01/11/1918	01/11/1918
War Diary	Reckem	01/11/1918	02/11/1918
War Diary	Mouscron	03/11/1918	18/03/1919
War Diary	Dunkerque	19/03/1919	26/03/1919
Heading	36th Division 108th Infy Bde 2nd Bn Roy. Irish Rif. Nov-Dec 1917 Feb 1918		
War Diary	In The Line	01/11/1917	08/11/1917
War Diary	Annequin	09/11/1917	10/11/1917
War Diary	Bethune	11/11/1917	12/11/1917
War Diary	Arras	13/11/1917	14/11/1917
War Diary	Ytres	15/11/1917	16/11/1917
War Diary	Barastre	17/11/1917	19/11/1917
War Diary	Lebucquiere	20/11/1917	20/11/1917
War Diary	In Field Hermies Moevres E.p.t 3 57 C	21/11/1917	21/11/1917
War Diary	In The Field	22/11/1917	22/11/1917
War Diary	In The Field Moeures	23/11/1917	23/11/1917
War Diary	In The Field	24/11/1917	24/11/1917
War Diary	In The Field Heroues	25/11/1917	25/11/1917
War Diary	In The Field	26/11/1917	26/11/1917
War Diary	Beaumetz	27/11/1917	27/11/1917
War Diary	Rocquigny	28/11/1917	29/11/1917
War Diary	Gommicourt	30/11/1917	01/12/1917
War Diary	Rocquigny	02/12/1917	02/12/1917
War Diary	Metz	03/12/1917	03/12/1917
War Diary	In The Field	04/12/1917	14/12/1917
War Diary	Metz	15/12/1917	15/12/1917
War Diary	Etricourt	16/12/1917	17/12/1917
War Diary	Warlincourt	18/12/1917	28/12/1917
War Diary	Gentelles	29/12/1917	06/01/1918

War Diary	Guillaucourt	07/01/1918	11/01/1918
War Diary	Herly And Billancourt	12/01/1918	13/01/1918
War Diary	Herly	13/01/1918	13/01/1918
War Diary	Pithon & Estouilly	14/01/1918	15/01/1918
War Diary	Fluquieres	16/01/1918	28/01/1918
War Diary	In The Field	29/01/1918	31/01/1918
War Diary	In The Line	01/02/1918	04/02/1918
War Diary	G.6.a. & c.	05/02/1918	07/02/1918
War Diary	In Dug Outs	08/02/1918	09/02/1918
War Diary	In The Line	10/02/1918	15/02/1918
War Diary	Fluquieres	16/02/1918	20/02/1918
War Diary	Gd. Seraucourt	21/02/1918	28/02/1918

WO95/2502/4.

36TH DIVISION
107TH INFY BDE

2ND BN ROY. IRISH RIF.
NOV FEB 1918-MAR 1919
FEB 1918

FROM 25 DIVISION
74 BDE

2nd BATTALION

THE ROYAL IRISH RIFLES

MARCH 1918

107th Brigade.
36th Division.

Volume 1, Sheet 1.

2R Irish Rif.

WAR DIARY
~~of~~
~~INTELLIGENCE SUMMARY~~
2nd Battalion, THE ROYAL IRISH RIFLES.
(Erase heading not required.)

MARCH, 1918.

Army Form C. 2118.

Place	Date	Hour	Summary of Events and Information (Ref.Map GRUGIES, 66 C.N.W.1, Edition, 2A.)	Remarks and references to Appendices
GRAND SERAUCOURT.	1st		Battalion relieved the 1st Royal Irish Rifles in Battle Zone. Battalion Headquarters remained at GRAND SERAUCOURT.	
"	2nd		Battalion working in Battle Zone.	
"	3rd.		Battalion working in Battle Zone.	
"	4th		Battalion working in Battle Zone.	
"	5th		Battalion working in Battle Zone.	
"	6th		Battalion relieved the 1st Royal Irish Rifles in the Line. "A" Company Left Front. "B" Company Right Front. "C" Company Passive Resistance Company, "D" Company Counter Attack Company. Battalion Headquarters in Railway Embankment, GRUIGES. Advanced Battalion Headquarters in QUARRY, B.14.a. Battalion holding line from B.8.c.80.20. Left Boundary, to B.10.c.40.50. Right Boundary.	
IN LINE	7th.		Battalion in the Line. Patrol consisting of 1 Officer and 20 Other Ranks sent out. 1 O.R. wounded in action.	
"	8th		Battalion in the line. Patrol consisting of 1 Officer and 20 Other Ranks sent out. 1 O.R. wounded in action.	
"	9th.		Battalion in the Line. 2 Other Ranks wounded in action.	
"	10th		Battalion in the Line. Inter-Company relief. "C" Company relieved "B" Company Right Front. "D" Company relieved "A" Company Left Front. "A" Company to Passive Resistance. "B" Company to Counter-attack. Enemy shelled Battalion front heavily for ten minutes at 9 p.m., again at 11 p.m. 4 O.Rs. wounded in action. 1 Other Rank Killed in action.	
"	11th		Battalion in the Line. Patrol of 1 Officer and 20 O.Rs. sent out. 1 Other Rank wounded in action. Enemy put down a bombardment along Battalion Front at 8 p.m. for 10 minutes.	
"	12th.		Battalion in the Line. Enemy bombardment at 5 a.m. for 10 minutes. 1 O.R. wounded in action.	
"	13th.		Battalion in the Line. Patrol consisting of 1 Officer and 20 O.Rs. sent out. 2 Other Ranks wounded in action.	
"	14th.		Battalion in the Line. Battalion relieved in the evening by 15th Bn. Royal Irish Rifles. Battalion moved to GRAND SERAUCOURT on completion of relief. "D" Company to SOMME Dugouts, "C" Company to HAMEL, and "A" and "B" Companies in GRAND SERAUCOURT. 2 Other Ranks wounded in action.	
GRAND SERAUCOURT.	15th		Battalion in Billets. Cleaning up, bathing, etc. Draft consisting of 104 Other Ranks joined.	
"	16th.		Battalion in Billets. Training commenced.	

(1)

Volume 1, Sheet 2.

WAR DIARY

~~INTELLIGENCE SUMMARY~~

2nd Battalion, THE ROYAL IRISH RIFLES.

(Erase heading not required.)

Army Form C. 2118.

Instructions regarding War Diaries and Intelligence Summaries are contained in F. S. Regs., Part II. and the Staff Manual respectively. Title pages will be prepared in manuscript.

Ref. Map, GRUIGES 66.c.N.W.1, 1/10,000

Place	Date	Hour	Summary of Events and Information	Remarks and references to Appendices
GRAND SERAUCOURT	17th		Battalion in Billets. St PATRICKS Day. Sports, etc. held.	
"	18th		Battalion in Billets. Training carried out. One Company on Range.	
"	19th		Battalion in Billets. Training carried out. One Company on Range.	
"	20th		Battalion Carried out training during morning. About 4 p.m. warning was received that the enemy was going to attack the following morning, Precautionary measures were taken.	
"	21st	5 am	Enemy bombardment of our front system and Battalion area which had been continuing intermittently throughout the night, became intensified	
"		6.30am	Order was received to "man Battle Stations", Companies moved independently to previously arranged points of assembly, Headquarters in QUARRY East of GRAND SERAUCOURT. LIEUT.C.R.W. McCAMMOND was wounded and gassed. About 10 a.m. 2/LIEUT.M.A.McFERRAN, M.C. was killed in the neighbourhood of GRUIGES, whilst endeavouring to ascertain the situation. 2 p.m. Orders were received to take up position along GRAND SERAUCOURT - ESSIGNY Road. This was done forthwith. The Battalion was not yet in contact with the enemy, but was being heavily shelled with both gas and H.E. shells. A thick mist rendered all observation exceedingly difficult. 4 p.m. Orders were received to assume former positions in QUARRY. 7 p.m. "D" Company in execution of previous orders advanced to CONTESCOURT to attempt to re-capture the Village. The enemy put up a stubborn resistence, and at the same time advanced to the attack, under cover of a very heavy gas shell bombardment. In spite of the utmost gallantry displayed by all ranks of "D" Company, no ground was gained. Very heavy losses were inflicted on the enemy, but both officers of "D" Company, LIEUT.G.E. LYNCH and 2/LIEUT.W.L.P.DOBBIN, M.C. were killed, and all the remainder of the Company, with the exception of about 40 O.Rs. became missing. Within a few minutes of the Company advancing to the attack, orders were received from O.C. 1st Royal Irish Rifles to cancel the assault, but these orders were not received in time to be acted on. 11.0p.m. The Battalion fell back by order of B.G.C. 107th Infantry Brigade on the LE HAMEL - HAPPENCOURT Road. Defensive positions were taken up, and the night passed quietly.	
LE HAMEL - HAPPENCOURT Road. Ref map. ST QUENTIN. 1/100,000.	22nd	11 am	The Battalion withdrew, under 107th Infantry Brigade orders, to an old French Trench system, South East of HAPPENCOURT. The mist had by this time cleared, and the enemy observing this movement shelled our troops on the move, but without inflicting many casualties.	

(2).

Volume 1, Sheet 3

WAR DIARY
of
~~INTELLIGENCE SUMMARY~~
2nd Battalion, THE ROYAL IRISH RIFLES.
(Erase heading not required.)

Army Form C. 2118.

Instructions regarding War Diaries and Intelligence Summaries are contained in F. S. Regs., Part II. and the Staff Manual respectively. Title pages will be prepared in manuscript.

Ref: Map. ST QUENTIN 1/100,000

Place	Date	Hour	Summary of Events and Information	Remarks and references to Appendices
LE HAMEL - HAPPENCOURT Road.	22nd (continued).		The Battalion remained here until dusk, the position was exceedingly difficult to hold, as the enemy had it under direct observation from the front. No troops were on our Right and there were no obstacles in front. 6 p.m. MAJOR R.de R.ROSE, M.C., who commanded the Battalion was wounded. At dusk the enemy, who had made some minor attacks during the afternoon, advanced in force, and orders were received to withdrew to SOMMETTE-EAUCOURT, via TUGNY and PITHON. On nearing SOMMETTE-EAUCOURT, information was received that the Battalion was to go to CUGNY, where the Battalion billetted. CAPT.T.J.C.C.THOMPSON, D.S.O. assumed command.	
CUGNY	23rd		A Draft of 67 Other Ranks joined the Battalion, together with various details from Courses, Leave, etc. The Battalion paraded and re-organised. 10 a.m. A defensive position North East of the Village was taken up. The remnants of "D" Company, together with reinforcements under the command of LIEUT.J.K.BOYLE, M.C. who rejoined the Battalion that morning, were in reserve North West of the Village. 12 noon. Reports were received that enemy patrols of cavalry had entered FLAVY le MARTEL and Brigade Orders directed that CUGNY was to be held at all costs. With the exception of one or two minor attacks, the afternoon passed quietly. Hostile aeroplanes were, however, very much in evidence. 6 p.m. The enemy attacked in force, but after a stiff fight was repulsed on our front, but later he succeeded in driving back the troops on the Right and he occupied positions between the Battalion and the Village. 8.30 p.m. A party of "C" Company under LIEUT.R.B.MARRIOTT-WATSON, M.C., which was returning to the Village, came in contact with a strong party of the enemy. LIEUT.R.B. MARRIOTT-WATSON, M.C. spoke to the enemy in German, and succeeded in allaying their suspicion, thus enabling the party to get to close quarters to rush and disperse the enemy. 10 p.m. The Battalion withdrew to a Line 300 yards West of the Village. No contact could be established with troops on either flanks. The night passed quietly, although the enemy could be heard, evidently in force, in the immediate front.	
CUGNY	24th	6 am	Touch was established with troops who had during the night moved forward. Enemy M.G. fire was very heavy during the morning, but no infantry advanced to the attack on the Battalion front, although on the right and left he succeeded in driving back our troops. Our flanks were slightly withdrawn to form defensive flanks. 2 p.m. The enemy advanced preceeded by a very heavy artillery bombardment in	

Volume 1, Sheet 5

Instructions regarding War Diaries and Intelligence Summaries are contained in F. S. Regs., Part II. and the Staff Manual respectively. Title pages will be prepared in manuscript.

WAR DIARY
of
~~INTELLIGENCE SUMMARY~~
2nd Battalion, THE ROYAL IRISH RIFLES.
(Erase heading not required.)

Army Form C. 2118.

Ref. map. ST.QUENTIN 1/100,000

Place	Date	Hour	Summary of Events and Information	Remarks and references to Appendices
	24th	(continued)	overwhelming strength, on our front and both flanks, and although the Battalion put up a most stubborn resistence, all with the exception of about 10 wounded O.R. and 10 unwounded were killed or taken prisoner. The following Officers became casualties during the day:- CAPT.T.J.C.C.THOMPSON,DSO Missing, CAPT.J.C.BRYANS, Missing, LIEUT. & A/Adjutant M.E.J.MOORE, M.C. Missing, LIEUT. R.B.MARRIOTT-WATSON, M.C. Missing, LIEUT.J.K.BOYLE, M.C. Missing, 2/LIEUT.E.C.STROHM, Missing.	
AVRICOURT Ref. map. AMIENS	25th		Various Officers and men who had returned from leave and courses, etc. and had been fighting with other units were collected and reorganised as a battalion. LIEUT-COL. P.G.A.COX, D.S.O. assumed command of this force which consisted of 8 Officers and 40 O.Rs. The Battalion moved the AVRICOURT where it was joined by the Transport, and bivouaced in a field.	
		6 p.m.	Orders were received to move to GUERBIGNY; this move was carried out partly by march route and partly by lorry, and was completed at 1.30 a.m. on 26th inst.	
GUERBIGNY	26th	11 am	The situation being somewhat obscure the Battalion, consisting of 4 Officers and 20 Other Ranks under the command of ~~MURRHY~~ CAPT.P.MURPHY, took up a defensive position between GUERBIGNY and ERCHES. 1st Bn. Royal Irish Rifles were on the Left, no troops on the immediate Right, but two Infantry Brigades and one French Cavalry Regiment were believed to be in front. The afternoon and evening passed quietly, but immediately after dark large columns of men and transport could be seen passing down the second class road from ERCHES - GUERBIGNY, about 100 yards to the Right of the position occupied by the Battalion. For some time these were believed to be French, but an Officer's Patrol got in touch with a Uhlan Patrol, and it was discovered they were enemy. About 9 p.m. rifle and machine gun fire, which had been much in evidence East of ERCHES died away, and at the same time Patrol sent from the Battalion to GUERBIGNY reported that the enemy held this place. The enemy thus being on three sides of the Battalion, Battalion moved to left and took up a position in rear of the 1st Battn. Royal Irish Rifles. The remainder of the night passed quietly although many enemy Patrols were met with.	
ERCHES.	27th	5.30 am	A Ration Party under C.Q.M.S. R.G.SOMERS missed it's way, and got into ERCHES Village, where it was twice charged by enemy Cavalry Patrols. The rations were however delivered, one man being wounded.	
		9 a.m.	The enemy attacked in force on three sides, after a short by severe fight the Battalion withdrew, first to a position 2000 yards North East of SAULCHOY sur DAVENSCOURT, and finally to a position East of HANTEST en SANTERRE. CAPT.P.MURPHY was wounded early in the operations, and LIEUT.C.O.CRAWFORD, M.C. assumed command.	

(4).

Sheet 5, Volume 1.

WAR DIARY
of
~~INTELLIGENCE SUMMARY.~~
2nd Battalion, THE ROYAL IRISH RIFLES.
(Erase heading not required.)

Army Form C. 2118.

Instructions regarding War Diaries and Intelligence Summaries are contained in F. S. Regs., Part II. and the Staff Manual respectively. Title pages will be prepared in manuscript.

Place	Date	Hour	Summary of Events and Information *Ref. map. AMIENS*	Remarks and references to Appendices
ERCHES	27	11.30 a.m.	The Battalion was relieved by 102ieme CHASSEURS ALPINS, and withdrew to SOURDON, where the Transport rejoined.	
	28	1 pm	Battalion under LIEUT-COL.P.G.A.COX, D.S.O. moved out and occupied a defensive position near COULLEMELLE the enemy was not met with.	
nr.COULLE-MELLE.	29		After a very wet and miserable night (28/29th) Battalion withdrew about 6 p.m. 29th to CHAUSSOY-EPARGNY.	
		9 p.m.	Battalion moved by march route to ORESMAUX and thence to lorry to VALLENNES, arriving about 6 a.m. on 30th inst.	
VALLENNES	30.	4.45 pm	The Battalion moved by march route to SALEUX where a miserable night was passed in the open.	
SALEUX	31.	9 am	The Battalion entrained and moved to GAMACHES (ref. map ABBEVILLE, 1/10,000) where it detrained and marched to MAISNIERES, arriving at about 4 p.m.	

TOTAL CASUALTIES DURING OPERATIONS:-

6 Officers Missing.   3 Officers Killed.   4 Officers Wounded.

616 O.Ranks Missing.   10 O.Ranks Killed.   64 O.Ranks Wounded.

12 O.Ranks wounded and missing.

(signed) LIEUT-COLONEL,
COMMANDING, 2nd BATTN. THE ROYAL IRISH RIFLES.

107th Brigade.
36th Division.

2nd BATTALION

THE ROYAL IRISH RIFLES

APRIL 1918.

VOLUME 2 - Sheet 1.

WAR DIARY of INTELLIGENCE SUMMARY.
2nd BATTN. THE ROYAL IRISH RIFLES.
(Erase heading not required.)

APRIL, 1918.

Army Form C. 2118.

Ref. SHEETS, DIEPPE and HAZEBROUCK 5a. Summary of Events and Information and SHEET 28 N.W., BELGIUM.

Place	Date	Hour	Summary of Events and Information
MAISNIERES	1st		Battalion in Billets. Kit, Arms and equipment inspections carried out.
"	2nd		Battalion in Billets. Draft of 9 Officers and 256 Other Ranks joined from Entrenching Battalions. Inspection of Box Respirators by Gas Expert.
"	3rd		Battalion in Billets. Re-organisation of Battalion carried out during morning.
		6 pm	Battalion paraded and marched to FEUQUIERES where it entrained about 9 p.m. for PROVEN (Flanders)
PROVEN	4th		Battalion arrived with transport at PROVEN Station where it detrained about 10 a.m.
		11 am	Battalion moved by Lorry to SEIGE CAMP at B.20.c.6.6. in the II Corps Area.
B.20.c.6.6.	5th		Battalion in Camp as above. Lecture in Camp Theatre by Army Commander.
	6th		Battalion proceeded to Line in POELCAPELLE Sector, relieving the 1st Gloucester Regt. in Left Sub-Sector.
POELCAPELLE	7th		Battalion in the Line. Patrols and work on improving trenches carried out.
Left-Sub-	8th		Battalion in the Line. Patrols and work on improving trenches carried out.
Sector.	9th		Battalion in the Line. Patrols and work on improving trenches carried out.
"	10th		Battalion in the Line. Patrols and work on improving trenches carried out.
"	11th		Battalion in the Line. Patrols and work on improving trenches carried out.
"	12th		Battalion in the Line. Patrols and work on improving trenches carried out. Night of 12/13th Battalion was relieved by 1st Bn. Royal Inniskilling Fusliers, and came back to man the Battle Zone. Battalion Headquarters established at BOCHCASTEL. Draft of 306 Other Ranks joined Details Camp.
BATTLE ZONE.	13th		Battalion in Battle Zone.
"	14th		Battn: in Battle Zone.
"	15th		Battalion in Battle Zone. During night 15/16th the 109th Brigade who were holding the Line withdrew through the Battalion leaving the Battalion to hold the line, which then became our Outpost Line.
"	16th		Battalion holding the Outpost Line.
"	17th		Battalion holding the Outpost Line. On night of 17/18th the Battalion was relieved by 2nd Bn. 18th Regiment of Belgians, and proceeded to SEIGE CAMP at B.20.c.6.6. 200 Other Ranks which joined Battalion on 12th inst. were sent back to II Corps Reinforcement Camp.
B.20.c.6.6.	18th		In morning interior economy carried out. In evening Lecture by G.O.C. Division to all ranks of the Battalion.
"	19th		In Camp. Training, re-equiping, re-organisation, etc. etc. carried out. TOTAL CASUALTIES for above tour in trenches: LT.J.CORDNER M.C. Killed in Action. 1 O.R. Accidentally killed, and 11 Other Ranks wounded in action.

(1).

VOLUME 2, SHEET 2.

Instructions regarding War Diaries and Intelligence Summaries are contained in F. S. Regs., Part II. and the Staff Manual respectively. Title pages will be prepared in manuscript.

WAR DIARY
of
~~INTELLIGENCE SUMMARY~~
2nd BATTN. THE ROYAL IRISH RIFLES.

APRIL, 1918.

Army Form C. 2118.

Place	Date	Hour	Ref. MAP, SHEET 28 N.W. BELGIUM. Summary of Events and Information	Remarks and references to Appendices
B.20.c.6.6.	20th		Battalion in Camp. During morning Company Commanders reconnoitred the Line. At 1 p.m. the Battalion proceeded by Companies to Support Line, relieving the 1st Bn. Royal Irish Rifles. The Battalion Headquarters established at FOCH FARM.	
FOCH FME.	21st		Battalion in Support Line.	
"	22nd		Battalion in Support Line. Enemy attack expected. All ranks were prepared for emergency.	
"	23rd	1 am	Battalion relieved 15th Royal Irish Rifles in Front Line. Battalion Headquarters was established in a Pill Box near HILL TOP FME.	
WEST OF STEENBEEK.	24th		Battalion in Outpost Line.	
"	25th		Battalion in Outpost Line. Work carried out in strengthening positions. Patrol sent out.	
"	26th		Battalion in Outpost Line. Work carried out in strengthening positions. Patrols sent out. 1 German officer & 2 O.Rs (Germans) captured by Patrol.	
"	27th		Battalion in Outpost Line. Work carried out in strengthening positions. Patrol sent out. Our Support Company relieved by 1st Royal Irish Rifles. At 3 a.m. the Battalion withdrew through 1st Bn. Royal Irish Rifles, leaving this Unit to hold the Outpost Line. Battalion then proceeded to WAGNER CAMP. Battalion Transport moved to Camp at about A.16.a.3.1.	
WAGNER CAMP.	28th		Battalion in Brigade Reserve at WAGNER CAMP. Work in Forward Area carried out. Draft of 10 O.Rs joined Details Camp.	
"	29th		Battalion in Reserve. Work in Forward Area carried out.	
"	30th		Battalion in Reserve. Work in Forward Area carried out. TOTAL CASUALTIES for above tour in Line:- CAPT.L.A.H.HACKETT, M.C. Killed in action 24.4.18, 2/LIEUT.V.E.GRANSDEN killed in action 26.4.18, 18 Other Ranks wounded in action.	

LIEUT-COLONEL,
COMMANDING, 2nd BATTN. THE ROYAL IRISH RIFLES.

VOLUME II, Sheet

MAY, 1918.

WAR DIARY
of
~~INTELLIGENCE SUMMARY~~
2nd BN: THE ROYAL IRISH RIFLES.
(Erase heading not required.)

Army Form C. 2118.

2nd R Irish Rifles

Vol R+Z

Instructions regarding War Diaries and Intelligence Summaries are contained in F. S. Regs., Part II. and the Staff Manual respectively. Title pages will be prepared in manuscript.

Ref: Maps SHEETS 28 N.W. BELGIUM, ST JULIEN, 1/10,000.

Place	Date	Hour	Summary of Events and Information	Remarks and references to Appendices
CANAL BANK.	1st		The Battalion relieved the 15th Bn. Royal Irish Rifles at CANAL BANK on night April 30th, 1918. One Company relieved a Company of the 1st Royal Irish Rifles at C.21.b.30.60. Battalion Headquarters at ESSEX FARM, C.25.a.20.90. An international post was found by the Battalion at BURNLEY, C.20.a.4.0. Working Parties furnished for 107th Infantry Brigade Headquarters.	
-do-	2nd		Battalion in Support, as above. Same Working Parties furnished.	
-do-	3rd		Battalion in Support as above. Same working parties furnished.	
-do-	4th		Battalion in Support as above. Same Working Parties furnished.	
-do-	5th		Battalion in Support as above. Same Working Parties furnished.	
-do-	6th		Battalion in Support as above. Same Working Parties furnished. On the night 6/7th the Battalion was relieved from CANAL BANK by the 1st Bn. Royal Irish Rifles, and proceeded to relieve the 15th Bn. The Royal Irish Rifles in the Outpost Line.	
IN THE LINE	7th		The Battalion holding the Line.	
-do-	8th		The Battalion holding the Line.	
-do-	9th		The Battalion holding the Line.	
-do-	10th		The Battalion holding the Line.	
-do-	11th		The Battalion holding the Line. On the night 11/12th May, 1918, the Battalion was relieved by the 15th Bn. The Royal Irish Rifles and proceeded to CANAL BANK EAST.	
CANAL BANK EAST.	12th		The Battalion in Support at CANAL BANK EAST. Work carried out in demolition East of CANAL. Carrying Parties furnished. Sundry other small working parties found daily.	
-do-	13th		The Battalion in Support as above. Working Parties as for previous day.	
-do-	14th		The Battalion in Support as above. Working Parties as for previous day.	
-do-	15th		The Battalion in Support as above. Working Parties as for previous day.	
-do-	16th		The Battalion in Support as above. Working Parties as for previous day.	
-do-,	17th		The Battalion in Support as above. Working Parties as for previous day. On the night 17/18th May, 1918, the Battalion was relieved by the 9th Bn. ROYAL IRSH FUSILIERS (108th Infantry Brigade) and withdrew to STEENJE CAMP (A.23.d.50.50) via BRIELEN and ELVERDINGHE. Battalion Headquarters proceeded to A.23.c.90.40.	
A.23.d.50.50.	18th		The Battalion in Divisional Reserve. Sunday - Divine Services held - all Denominations. Kit, Arms, clothing and box respirator inspections carried out. Total Casualties for last tour in Line, 2/LIEUT. E.A.COCHRANE, Wounded in action, 4 Other Ranks Killed in Action, 7 Other Ranks Wounded in Action.	

VOLUME III, Sheet 2.

WAR DIARY
of
~~INTELLIGENCE SUMMARY~~
2nd BN. THE ROYAL IRISH RIFLES.

Army Form C. 2118.

Place	Date	Hour	Summary of Events and Information	Remarks and references to Appendices
STEENJE CAMP, A.23.d. 50.50.	19th		The Battalion in Divisional Reserve. Three hours training carried out under Company arrangements in vicinity of Camp. Battalion proceeded to Baths.	
	20th		The Battalion in Divisional Reserve. Working parties furnished for work on the GREEN LINE, B.26.b.2.9. Training carried out by remainder of the Battalion. CAPT. J. ARNOTT admitted to Hospital. R.Q.M.S. A. CONNON promoted HON. LIEUT. & QUARTERMASTER.	
- do -	21st		Battalion in Divisional Reserve. On this date the whole Battalion was engaged in work on the GREEN LINE about B.26.b.2.9.	
- do -	22nd		Battalion in Divisional Reserve. On this date the whole Battalion was engaged in work on the GREEN LINE about B.26.b.2.9.	
- do -	23rd		Battalion in Divisional Reserve. Training carried out. Musketry, Arms drill, Fire control, Gas drill, Platoon Drill, etc: etc:	
- do -	24th		Battalion in Divisional Reserve. Two Companies carried out work on the GREEN LINE and two Companies carried out training in vicinity of Camp.	
- do -	25th		Battalion in Divisional Reserve. Working Parties and Training same as for previous day.	
- do -	26th		Battalion in Divisional Reserve - Sunday - Divine Services held for all Denominations. No training or work was carried out on this date. Battalion Sports were held in the afternoon on Football Field. The Divisional Band was in attendance.	
- do -	27th		Battalion in Divisional Reserve. Training carried out.	
- do -	28th		Battalion in Divisional Reserve. Two Companies engaged on work on the GREEN LINE, two Companies training in the vicinity of Camp, Box Respirator inspection carried out by Gas Expert. Battalion proceeded by Companies to Baths at INTERNATIONAL CORNER.	
- do -	29th		Battalion in Divisional Reserve. Bathing continued. Notification was received that the following Officer, Warrant officer and man had been mentioned in SIR D. HAIG'S Despatch:- MAJOR C.W. GARNER, Company Sergeant Major D. FERRIS, and No.8235 Rifleman HUTCHISON G. (killed). STEENJE Camp, which the Battalion occupied, assumed the name of SEABORN CAMP from this date. The Battalion relieved the 9th ROYAL IRISH FUSILIERS (108th Infantry Brigade) in the RIGHT SUB-SECTOR on the night 29/30th May, 1918. Battalion proceeded by RAILWAY TRAIN (LIGHT) to Line, entraining at SEABORN CAMP (STEENJE CAMP) at 8 p.m.	

VOLUME III, Sheet 3.

WAR DIARY of
~~INTELLIGENCE SUMMARY~~
2nd BN. THE ROYAL IRISH RIFLES.
(Erase heading not required.)

Army Form C. 2118.

Place	Date	Hour	Summary of Events and Information	Remarks and references to Appendices
RIGHT SUB-SECTOR.	30th		Battalion holding Outpost Line in RIGHT SUB-SECTOR	
- do -	31st		Battalion holding Outpost Line in RIGHT SUB-SECTOR.	

Casualties for last two days:- 1 Other Rank wounded in action.

NOTE: During the month an Instructional Class was established under the supervision of MAJOR C.W. GARNER at the Battalion Transport Lines where, under selected N.C.O. Instructors, untrained men of recent Reinforcements, partially trained Signallers and Lewis Gunners, received instruction for one fortnight, when they were replaced by others from the Battalion.

S T R E N G T H.

Total Strength of Battalion ... 35½ Officers ... 1140 Other Ranks.

Actually with Battalion ... 22 Officers ... 784 Other Ranks.

Lieut-Colonel,
Commanding, 2nd Battn. The Royal Irish Rifles.

VOLUME IV Sheet 1

JUNE 1918

Army Form C. 2118.

WAR DIARY
of
INTELLIGENCE SUMMARY
2nd BN: THE ROYAL IRISH RIFLES.
(Erase heading not required.)

Instructions regarding War Diaries and Intelligence Summaries are contained in F. S. Regs., Part II. and the Staff Manual respectively. Title pages will be prepared in manuscript.

Ref. Maps.
Sheet 28.N.W.BELGIUM
Sheet St JULIEN 1/10,000

Vol 43

Place	Date	Hour	Summary of Events and Information	Remarks and references to Appendices
RIGHT SUB-SECTOR	1st		Battalion was holding Outpost Line in Right Sub-Sector - Precautionary patrols were sent out in the early hours of morning. Work on strengthening defences carried out. 1 Other Rank was accidentally killed whilst investigation of a stoppage in a Lewis Gun was being carried out.	
-do-	2nd		Battalion holding Outpost Line in Right Sub-Sector. At midnight a reconnaissance patrol was sent out under the Battalion Intelligence Officer (2nd Lt.N.B.MUNN) consisting of 5 O.Ranks G.S.O. II of II Corps Headquarters also accompanied this patrol. The object of this patrol was to reconnoitre the road in C.23.c. and C.29.b. and to endeavour to locate a suspected enemy post at C.29.b.50.90. The party left our Outpost Line at C.29.a.30.85 and proceeded along Light Railway to C.23.c.20.10 thence up track No.5 to C.23.c.23.35 and along road - At about C.23.d.40.10. the patrol was heavily bombed and G.S.O.II of II Corps (MAJOR H. MUSGRAVE R.E's) was killed - at this juncture the patrol scattered and took cover in shell holes - 2nd Lt.MUNN personally carried the body of MAJOR MUSGRAVE towards our lines but fell exhausted about half way, having been himself wounded in about 12 places - with the aid of 2nd Lieuts H.MARSHALL and 2nd L.J.RICKS the body was brought back to our lines - 3 Other Ranks of the patrol were also wounded. No enemy were seen.	
-do-	3rd		Battalion holding Outpost Line in Right Sub-Sector - precautionary patrols sent out. Work on strengthening positions continued.	
-do-	4th		Battalion holding Outpost Line in Right Sub-Sector - precautionary Patrols sent out. Work on strengthening positions continued.	
-do-	5th		Battalion holding Outpost Line in Right Sub-Sector. Night 5/6th Battalion was relieved by 3rd Battalion, 4th Carabineers plus one Company of the 2nd Battalion 4th Carabineers. See Operation Order No.34 attached. On completion of relief the Battalion proceeded to READING STATION, B.22.d.30.30, where troops entrained for KOUTEK, E.28.c. On detraining, Battalion marched to Corps Reserve Billets at ROAD CAMP, F.25.d. (SHEET 27).	
ROAD-CAMP	6th	8.30am	Battalion arrived at ROAD CAMP.	
		2 PM	Battalion in Corps Reserve. General cleaning up carried out. Total casualties sustained during last tour in trenches:- Major H.Musgrave, D.S.O., Royal Engineers (G.S.O.2, II Corps), KILLED. 2/LIEUT.N.B.MUNN, WOUNDED. 7 Other Ranks, WOUNDED. 1 O.R. ACCIDENTALLY KILLED	

June 1918

WAR DIARY of INTELLIGENCE SUMMARY.

2nd Bn The Royal Irish Rifles

(Erase heading not required.)

Army Form C. 2118.

Sheet 28 NW BELGIUM
ST JULIEN 1/10,000

Place	Date	Hour	Summary of Events and Information	Remarks and references to Appendices
ROAD CAMP	7th		Battalion in Corps Reserve at ROAD CAMP. At Reveille, the Details undergoing instruction at the Transport Lines, rejoined the Battalion. Sundry inspections carried out under Company arrangements. Commencement of training.	
- do -	8th		Battalion in training. Representatives sent to reconnoitre BLUE Line. The Commanding Officer inspected the Battalion by Companies.	
- do -	9th		Battalion in Corps Reserve. (Sunday) Divine Services held for all Denominations.	
- do -	10th	10 am	Battalion was to be inspected by the Corps Commander, Lieut-General Sir Claud Jacob, K.C.B. and carried out a rehearsal together with the other units of the 107th Infantry Brigade.	
		2 pm	Battalion paraded with remainder of the Brigade for above inspection but owing to the inclement weather the troops returned to Billets and the Corps Commander interviewed all Officers.	
- do -	11th		Battalion carried out training in vicinity of billets and musketry training on the range. Lieut.C.O.Crawford, M.C. left Battalion to proceed to India Office, London. Capt. R.A. Young M.C. appointed Acting Adjutant. Major H.Clendining assumed duties of Second-in-Command. Major C.W. Garner took over command of "C" Company.	
- do -	12th		Training carried out. On this date the Divisional Gas Officer put the Battalion through a Gas Test.	
- do -	13th		Battalion after completing work on the BLUE Line proceeded to PETERBOROUGH CAMP in the PROVEN Area.	
PETERBOROUGH CAMP.	14th		Battalion engaged on work on the BLUE Line, excepting a few Lewis Gunners who carried out training in the vicinity of Camp.	
- do -	15th		Sunday. No work carried out. Divine Services held. At this period it was expected that the II Corps Front would be attacked, and all preliminary arrangements were made to meet any suprise of this nature.	
- do -	16th		Battalion engaged on work on BLUE Line.	
- do -	17th		Battalion engaged in work on BLUE Line. Lieut.C.R.W.McCAMMOND and 2/LIEUT.J.N.G.STEWART joined Battalion. LIEUT.T.H.WITHEROW was transferred to the Indian Army. 2/LIEUT.F. BRADLEY was invalided to England Sick. LIEUT.T.G.HENDERSON proceeded to Machine Gun Corps England, and notification was received that LIEUT.C.O.CRAWFORD, M.C. was appointed Acting Captain and Adjutant to the Battalion.	
- do -	18th		Battalion continued work on the BLUE Line. 3 Other Ranks joined the Battalion.	
- do -	19th		Battalion continued work on the BLUE Line. On this date 2/LIEUT.L.H.PROCTOR proceeded to England to join the R.A.F.	

(2).

WAR DIARY
2nd BN. THE ROYAL IRISH RIFLES.

Army Form C. 2118.

Sheet 28 NW BELGIUM
ST JULIEN 1/10,000

Place	Date	Hour	Summary of Events and Information	Remarks and references to Appendices
PETERBOROUGH CAMP	20th		The Battalion continues work on the BLUE Line.	
TUNNELLERS CAMP.	21st		The Battalion left PETERBOROUGH CAMP and marched to TUNNELLERS CAMP. On this date the G.O.C. 36th Division Lectured to all Officers at 107th Infantry Brigade Headquarters.	
- do -	22nd		The Battalion carried out intensive training. All Lewis Gunners fired on the Range in TUNNELLERS CAMP.	
- do -	23rd		Sunday. Divine Services held.	
- do -	24th		The Battalion moved to the CASSEL and RUBROUCK Areas for Musketry Training. The Administrative Portion of the Battalion remained at TUNNELLERS CAMP.	
CASSEL AND RUBROUCK Area	25th		The Battalion carried out Musketry Training. Two Companies were at CASSEL and two at RUBROUCK	
- do -	26th		Musketry training continued.	
- do -	27th		Musketry Training continued.	
TUNNELLERS CAMP.	28th		The Battalion left the CASSEL and RUBROUCK Areas and returned to TUNNELLERS CAMP. Two Companies moved by Train, and two by March Route.	
- do -	29th		Battalion training.	
- do -	30th		Battalion Training.	

STRENGTH. STRENGTH WITH BATTALION.

OFFICERS ... 33   OFFICERS ... 22

OTHER RANKS ... 1,100.   OTHER RANKS ... 796.

Lieut-Colonel,
Commanding, 2nd BN. THE ROYAL IRISH RIFLES

Volume V
Sheet 1.

WAR DIARY of
~~INTELLIGENCE SUMMARY~~
2nd BN. THE ROYAL IRISH RIFLES.
(Erase heading not required.)

JULY, 1918

Army Form C. 2118.

Instructions regarding War Diaries and Intelligence Summaries are contained in F. S. Regs., Part II, and the Staff Manual respectively. Title pages will be prepared in manuscript.

Reference Maps:-
Sheet 28 N.W. Belgium
HAZEBROUCK 5a
Berthen & Meteren (Ed. 4a Local sheets)
Sheet 27 S.E. (Eastern half)

Place	Date	Hour	Summary of Events and Information	Remarks and references to Appendices
TUNNELLERS CAMP.	1st		The Battalion was billetted in TUNNELLERS CAMP. The Battalion paraded under R.S.M. in morning. 36th Divisional Horse Show and Sports held on this date near the village of PROVEN.	
-do-	2nd		The Battalion carried out training in TUNNELLERS CAMP. Inspection of men's kits, arms and accoutrements held.	
P.32.c.2.7.	3rd		The Battalion paraded at 6-40 a.m. and proceeded by march route to CASSEL AREA, arriving at a Camp about P.32.c.2.7. by 11-40 a.m. The remainder of the day was devoted to interior economy, foot inspection, etc., etc..	
-do-	4th		The Battalion carried out training in vicinity of Billets, also Lewis Gun practice on Ranges near Camp.	
-do-	5th		The Battalion in camp as yesterday. On this date advance parties, consisting of C.O., Sigs.Offr and Intelligence Offr, 1 Officer and 4 N.C.O's per Company proceeded to Line to reconnoitre the positions in the SCHAEXKEN-FONTAINE HOUCK Line to be taken over by the Battalion on night 6/7th. This party EXCEPT FOR THE C.O. remained in the Line until arrival of Battalion, when they acted as Guides. On this date LIEUT. K.D. LESLIE proceeded to ENGLAND and was struck off the strength of the Battalion.	
-do-	6th	Morn.	The Battalion in Camp at P.32.c.2.7. Companies on this date were at the disposal of Company Commanders. Divine service for Roman Catholics held at 8 a.m. in the PARISH CHURCH HONDINGHEM.	
		Eve.	The Battalion proceeded to the Line and relieved the 128th Infantry Regiment of the FRENCH ARMY., in the Support Line. The Battalion moved to Q.23.a.20.30., The surplus personnel under MAJOR H.CLENDINING moved to H.30.a. LIEUT.R.C.SCOTT struck off strength of Battalion. Authy: Second Army No.D/321/845/dated 25.6.1918.	

(1)

Volumn V
Sheet II

Army Form C. 2118.

WAR DIARY

of

~~INTELLIGENCE SUMMARY~~
2nd BN: THE ROYAL IRISH RIFLES.
(Erase heading not required.)

JULY 1918

Instructions regarding War Diaries and Intelligence Summaries are contained in F. S. Regs., Part II. and the Staff Manual respectively. Title pages will be prepared in manuscript.

Place	Date	Hour	Reference Map:- (See p.p. 1) Summary of Events and Information	Remarks and references to Appendices
Support Line FONTAINE SCHAEXKEN HOUCK	7th		The Battalion holding Support Line in the Right Brigade Sector. (SCHAEXKEN - FONTAINE HOUCK) Working parties, after dark, engaged on cutting crops, digging trenches, revetting, wiring, etc in Support Line. Parties were also found for work under the 15th (S) Bn. The Royal Irish Rifles.	
--do--	8th		The Battalion holding Support Line in the Right Brigade Sector. Working parties, after dark, engaged on cutting crops, digging trenches, revetting, wiring, etc in Support Line. Parties were also found for work under the 15th (S) Bn. The Royal Irish Rifles.	
--do--	9th		The Battalion holding Support Line in Right Brigade Sector. Same working parties found as for yesterday.	
--do--	10th		The Battalion holding Support Line in Right Brigade Sector. Same working parties found as for yesterday. LIEUT.C.R.W.McCAMMOND Wounded in Action. On this date Lieut-Colonel P.G.A.COX.D.S.O. proceeded to ENGLAND, to the Senior Officers' School, ALDERSHOT and MAJOR H.CLENDINING took over command of the Battalion.	
--do--	11th		The Battalion holding Support Line in Right Brigade Sector. Same working parties found as for yesterday.	
--do--	12th		The Battalion holding Support Line in Right Brigade Sector. Same working parties found as for yesterday. Captain R.WATTS.M.C. , Lieut.F.L.BATTERSHILL.M.C. , LIEUT.A.ROLLINGS M.C. and LIEUT R.C.SCOTT joined the Battalion on this date. LIEUT.R.A.O'NEILL struck off strength of Battalion on being pronounced B III at HAVRE, by a Medical Board.	
--do--	13th		The Battalion holding Support Line in Right Brigade Sector Same working parties found as for yesterday.	
--do--	14th		The Battalion holding Support Line in Right Brigade Sector. Same working parties found as for yesterday.	

Volume V
Sheet iii

WAR DIARY of ~~INTELLIGENCE SUMMARY~~
2nd BN: THE ROYAL IRISH RIFLES.

JULY 1918

Army Form C. 2118.

Place	Date	Hour	Map reference:- (see p.p.i) Summary of Events and Information	Remarks and references to Appendices
Support Line SCHAEXKEN -FONTAINE HOUCK.	15th		The dispositions of the Battalion in Support having been changed and the frontage widened the Battalion took over more line from the 1st Bn. The Royal Irish Rifles, the Battle positions now extending from FONTAINE HOUCK on the right to HERMITAGE on the left. The Company dispositions were as follows:- "A" Company on the Right - "B" Company Right centre - "D" Company Left centre and "C" Company left. "C" Company becoming nucleus garrison company. In addition to these dispositions, one Company from 15th (S) Bn. The Royal Irish Rifles (relieved on this night by the 1st Bn. The Royal Irish Rifles.) took up position as a nucleus garrison between "A" and "B" Company. Battalion Headquarters were in MANCHE COPSE. 1/4 R.29.c.50.45. "A" Company were in Farm at X.4.a.50.25. "B" Company were in Farm at R.34.c.25.00. "C" Company were in Farm at R.35.b.50.35. "D" Company in Farm at R.35.a.30.50.	
Support Line FONTAINE HOUCK ERMITAGE.	16th		The Battalion holding Support Line. Working parties found for cutting crops, wiring, revetting digging trenches, etc,. etc,. LIEUT. A. COLLINGS. M.C. was Wounded in Action on this date. LIEUT. F.L. BATTERSHILL was admitted to Field Ambulance "Sick" on this date.	
-do-	17th		The Battalion holding Support Line. Working parties found as for yesterday. During the day 30 men were able to get bathed in improvised baths erected in the Battalion Sector. Clean changes of underclothing having been sent up from Rear Battalion Headquarters the night previous.	
-do-	18th		The Battalion holding Support Line. Working parties found as for yesterday. On this date Captain R. WATTS. M.C. took over command and payment of "C" Company from Lieut. V.C. YOUNG.	

Volume V
Sheet IV

WAR DIARY of
~~INTELLIGENCE SUMMARY~~
2nd BN. THE ROYAL IRISH RIFLES.

Army Form C. 2118.

July 1918

Place	Date	Hour	Map Reference:- (see p.p.i) Summary of Events and Information	Remarks and references to Appendices
FONTAINE HOUCK ERMITAGE Support Line	19th		The Battalion holding the Support Line. The following working party was found - 2 Officers and 100 Other Ranks from Companies- This party was engaged on work under the 1st Bn.The Royal Irish Rifles in Front and immediate Support Lines. Local work done nightly by Companies to Trenches and shelters in their respective areas.	
-do-	20th		The Battalion holding the Support Line. The same work began yesterday was carried on to-day.	
-do-	21st		The Battalion holding the Support Line. As yesterday, work was continued.	
-do-	22nd		The Battalion holding the Support Line. Working parties continued with the tasks allotted to them on 19th inst.	
-do-			Details under 2nd Lieut.J.N.S.Stewart rejoined the Battalion and another class of Instruction under Capt.R.O.MANSERGH proceeded from the Line to Rear Battalion Headquarters. Remaining at this latter place overnight, they proceeded next day to the Details Camp near BAVINCHOVE.	
-do-	23rd.		The Battalion holding the Support Line. Work on trenches and dug-outs continued.(Details under Capt.R.O.MANSERGH moved to MONNINGUES) Night 23rd/24th the Battalion relieved the 1st Bn.The Royal Irish Rifles in the Front Line system, being relieved in the Support Line by the 15th (S) Bn.The Royal Irish Rifles.	
Front Line Bn.H.Q. at KOPJE FARM X.5.a. 55.20.	24th		The Battalion holding Brigade Front.Dispositions as follows:- "A" Company, Right front. "C" Company left front with Company Headquarters at HAUTE PORTE FME and SALVO FME respectively. "B" Company in Counter attack. "D" Company in Reserve with Company Headquarters at RISKY FARM and RUNAWAY FARM respectively. After dark Working parties were engaged on digging trenches, cutting crops, wiring, revetting, etc The Brigade frontage - Right, X.11.c.55.15 - Left, S.1.c.50.15. The following Officers joined the Battalion on this date:- LIEUT.C.H.DEACON - 2nd LIEUT. J.M.WRIGHT - 2nd Lieut.F.K.McKEHMAN.	

Volume V
Sheet V.

WAR DIARY of INTELLIGENCE SUMMARY.
2nd BN: THE ROYAL IRISH RIFLES.
(Erase heading not required.)

Army Form C. 2118.

JULY 1918

Instructions regarding War Diaries and Intelligence Summaries are contained in F. S. Regs., Part II. and the Staff Manual respectively. Title pages will be prepared in manuscript.

Map references:- See p.p.1.

Place	Date	Hour	Summary of Events and Information	Remarks and references to Appendices
KOPJE FARM Y.5.a. 55.20.	25th		Battalion holding front line. Work carried on as for yesterday.	
	26th		Battalion holding front line. Work carried on as for yesterday.	
-do-	27th		Battalion holding front Line. Work carried out as for yesterday. On this date there was and inter-Company relief. Dispositions were as follows after the relief was complete. "B" Company Right Front. "D" Company Left Front. "A" Company. Counter attack. "C" Company Reserve.	
-do-	28th		Battalion holding Front Line. Work carried out as for yesterday.	
-do-	29th		Battalion holding front line. The same work was carried on. At 5-30 p.m on this date a patrol was sent out under LIEUT.D.B.WALKINGTON and 2nd LIEUT.J.N.G.STEWART composed of 4 Other Ranks with the object of obtaining identification. The patrol left our Line at X.11.b.68.02. and made direct for X.12.c.o1.23. At this point a German post was found the patrol rushed the post which appeared to be held by about ten men. 4 prisoners were taken.(1.N.C.O. and three men) 2 of whom were killed in NO MAN'S LAND on the way back as they shewed fight,when enemy machine gun opened fire. The remainder of the post were either killed or wounded. At this juncture the patrol was fired on by enemy Machine gun but no casualties occurred. The patrol re-entered our Line at 7-45 p.m. at about X.12.c.28.16.	
-do-	30th		Battalion holding the front Line. Same work was continued on trenches,etc. On this date the enemy shelled our front rather heavily,especially the Headquarters of "B" Company where he inflicted some casualties. LIEUT.E.MORROW was wounded on this date.	
-do-	31st.		Battalion holding front Line. Work as usual carried on. On the night 31st July/1st Aug. the Battalion was relieved in the front Line by the 15th (S) Bn.The ROYAL IRISH RIFLES and on relief proceeded to quarters vacated by the 1st Bn.THE ROYAL IRISH RIFLES and became Battalion in Brigade Reserve,and commenced work on the BLUE LINE.	

H. Clendining MAJOR.,
1.8.1918. Commanding., 2nd BN: THE ROYAL IRISH RIFLES.

VOL: 6
SHEET 1.

WAR DIARY
of
~~INTELLIGENCE SUMMARY~~
2nd BN. THE ROYAL IRISH RIFLES.
Sh. 28. N.W. Belgium.
(Erase heading not required)

AUGUST 1918

Army Form C. 2118.

Instructions regarding War Diaries and Intelligence Summaries are contained in F. S. Regs., Par. II. and the Staff Manual respectively. Title pages will be prepared in manuscript.

Place	Date	Hour	Ref: Maps:- Berthen & Meteren.	Hazebrouck 5 a Sh. 27 S.E. & 28 S.W. Sheet 27. Summary of Events and Information	Remarks and references to Appendices
WIGWAM COPSE	1st	4a.m.		Battalion arrived at WIGWAM COPSE - Dispositions as follows:- "A" Company at TIBETS FM. "B" Company in Farm at NOOTE BOOM "C" Company at ROBERTS FARM - "D" Company at SENLAC FM. Battalion took over work on BLUE LINE from 1st Bn. The Royal Irish Rifles.	
-do-	2nd			Battalion in Brigade Reserve - Work carried out at night on BLUE LINE under R.E's During the day "C" Company's Headquarters at ROBERTS FM was heavily shelled.	
-do-	3rd			Battalion in Brigade Reserve. Work on BLUE LINE continued. 20 Other Ranks rejoined the Battalion on 'Turnover scheme' from the 36th Divisional Reception Camp. 50 Other Ranks left the Battalion to join the Divisional Reception Camp.	
-do-	4th			Battalion in Brigade Reserve - Work on BLUE LINE continued. A party consisting of 3 Officers 15 men and 1 Bugler proceeded to TERDEGHEM CHURCH to attend Anniversary Service of the outbreak of the War. On this date only half the Battalion was engaged on work - the other half were able to get bathed at the Baths at PIEBROUCK.	
-do-	5th			Battalion in Brigade Reserve- Work on BLUE LINE continued. Only half the Battalion was required for work the other half making use of the Baths at PIEBROUCK. On this date there was an Inter-Company relief carried out. "C" Company relieving "D" Company.	
-do-	6th			Battalion in Brigade Reserve- On this date every available man in the Battalion was engaged working on the BLUE LINE.	
-do-	7th			Battalion in Brigade Reserve - Work carried out as yesterday on the BLUE LINE. LIEUT. J.N. INGLIS and party of 30 Other Ranks rejoined the Battalion from Divisional Reception Camp. The following Officers joined the Battalion - CAPTAIN W.B. TEELE - LIEUT. A.E. BUTTLE.	
-do-	8th			Battalion was relieved in Brigade Reserve Sector by the 15th (S) Battn. The Royal Irish Rifles. and proceeded to relieve the 1st Bn. The Royal Irish Rifles in the Support Line. The dispositions of the Battalion were now as follows:- Battalion Headquarters at LA MANCHE COPSE at R.29 c.50.45. - "A" Company (nucleus garrison) at FM R.35.b.50.85. - "B" Company at VANILLA FM. "C" Company at FM. X.4.a.45.35. - "D" Company at ROBERTS FARM.	

VOL: 6
Sheet 2.

WAR DIARY
of
~~INTELLIGENCE SUMMARY~~
2nd BN. THE ROYAL IRISH RIFLES.

Army Form C. 2118.

AUGUST 1918.

Instructions regarding War Diaries and Intelligence Summaries are contained in F. S. Regs., Part II. and the Staff Manual respectively. Title pages will be prepared in manuscript.

Place	Date	Hour	Map Ref. (See p.p.1.) Summary of Events and Information	Remarks and references to Appendices
LA MANCHE COPSE	9th		Battalion holding Support Line from FONTAINE HOUCK on the right to ERMITAGE on the left in the 107th Infantry Brigade Sector. Work on the BLUE LINE was continued until 2 a.m. 10th inst when all work on the BLUE LINE was taken over by the 15th (S) Bn.The Royal Irish Rifles.	
-do-	10th		Battalion holding Support Line. On this date "D" Company supplied working parties for work in the front line under the R.E.'s. "A" "C" and "D" Companies worked on improvement of their respective Sectors. On this date 2nd Lieut.R.A.GOUGH and 10 selected Other Ranks of the Battalion attended a Special Divine Service at Divisional Headquarters at TERDEGHEM and were afterwards on parade when HIS MAJESTY THE KING was inspecting troops in the Second Army Area. 50 Other Ranks on 'turnover scheme' rejoined the Battalion with 9 Other Ranks reinforcements 50 Other Ranks from the Battalion proceeded to Divisional Reception Camp. LIEUT.W.McCOY joined the Battalion. Captain R.WATTS.M.C. took over the duties of Acting Adjutant to the Battalion from Lieut.R.A.YOUNG.M.C. who proceeded on Leave to U.K. LIEUT.J.N.INGLIS took over command and payment of "C" Company from this date. Working parties carried out work under the R.E's.	
-do-	11th.		Battalion holding Support Line. Work carried on under the R.E's. LIEUT.H.G.HARMER and 2nd LIEUT.F.T.POOLE joined the Battalion.	
-do-	12th		Battalion holding Support Line. Work carried on under R.E.s. Party of 88 Other Ranks proceeded to 36th Divisional Training Camp at BONNINGUES and 92 Other Ranks rejoined the Battalion from that Camp.	
-do-	13th		Battalion holding Support Line. Working parties worked under R.E.s.	
-do-	14th		Battalion holding Support Line. Working parties continued work under R.E's. On this date the area which the Battalion was responsible for was heavily Gas shelled and more especially the vicinity of "A" Company's Headquarters. The following casualties occurred:- Captain C.E.BARTON 2nd Lieut.C.H.LANE and 2ndLts R.A.GOUGH & F.T.POOLE were Gassed. Captain C.E.BARTON and 2nd Lt.LANE later succumbed to the effects of the Gas. Approximately 60 Other Ranks were also gassed. That night one half of the Battalion obtained a bath at the PIEBROUCK BATHS.	
-do-	15th		Battalion holding Support Line. One half of the Battalion was engaged on work and the other half were able to obtain a bath. 2nd Lieut.R.GREACEN joined the Battalion.	
-do-	16th		Battalion holding Support Line. On this date the Battalion was relieved in the Support Line and not waiting to be relieved by 1st Bn.The Royal Irish Rifles proceeded to the 108th Infantry Brigade Sector relieving the 9th (N.I.H.)Royal Irish Fusiliers in 108th Brigade Left front line Sector.	

Vol: 6
Sheet 3.

Instructions regarding War Diaries and Intelligence Summaries are contained in F. S. Regs., Par. II. and the Staff Manual respectively. Title pages will be prepared in manuscript.

WAR DIARY of
~~INTELLIGENCE SUMMARY~~.
2nd BN. THE ROYAL IRISH RIFLES.
(Erase heading not required.)

Army Form C. 2118.

AUGUST 1918

Place	Date	Hour	Map Refs:- (See p.p.1.) Summary of Events and Information	Remarks and references to Appendices
LEFT BDE FRONT LINE SECTOR.	17th		Battalion holding Left Brigade Front Line Sector being attached to the 108th Infantry Brigade for tactical purposes and to the 107th Infantry Brigade for administration. Every available man was sent to the Front Line Companies for work on strengthening same and for cutting crops in front of the Front Line. This work was carried out at about X.2.c.20.65 - S.1.d.90.25. - S.2.d.4.2. to S.3.c.1.1. On this date Captain W.M.DOWNING joined the Battalion.	
-do-	18th		Battalion holding the Front Line in above Sector. On this date the line was heavily shelled. Party of 60 Other Ranks joined the Battalion from the Divisional Reception Camp. LIEUT.W.H.CALWELL joined the Battalion on this date. Work carried out as yesterday.	
-do-	19th		Battalion holding Front Line. Work on Front Line and cutting crops continued. That night a special task of erecting a new belt of wire at S.2.d.7.3. and at S.2.d.9.3. was carried out.	
-do-	20th		Battalion holding Front Line in Left Brigade Sector. Work as on the 19th continued.	
-do-	21st		Battalion relieved by 1st Bn.THE ROYAL IRISH RIFLES in Front Line and proceeded to Support Line of the 107th Infantry Brigade. Dispositions as follows:- Battalion Headquarters at LA MANCHE COPSE. R.29.c.50.45. - "A" Company at VANILLA FARM - "B" Company (nucleus garrison) at ROBERTS FARM - "D" Company at BLIGHTY FARM.	."C" Coy (R.35.b.50.85.)
SUPPORT LINE MANCHE COPSE R.29.c. 50.45.	22nd		Battalion in Support Line in 107th Infantry Brigade Sector. Battalion engaged on work on the BLUE LINE. Parties sent to Baths at PIEBROUCK.	
	23rd		Battalion holding Support Line as yesterday. Same work carried on as on 22nd inst.	
	24th		Battalion in Support Line. Sundry Working Parties engaged on tasks under supervision of R.E's. 50 Other Ranks joined the Battalion from the Divisional Reception Camp and 50 Other Ranks joined the Divisional Reception Camp from the Battalion. On this night the vicinity of Battalion Headquarters was shelled with Gas shells. The Battalion assisted in digging a new Front Line together with the 16th Bn.The Royal Irish Rifles (P). The following casualties occurred:- 2nd LIEUT.R.I.JOHNSTON wounded and LIEUT.W.H.CALWELL was wounded. The following Officers joined the Battalion. LIEUT.H.D.CUMMINGS 2nd LIEUT.H.D.MITCHELL and 2nd LIEUT. W.EATON. Captain A.ANDERSON.RAMC became attached to the Battalion for duties as Medical Officer during the absence of Captain G.E.LINDSAY.M.C.RAMC on Leave.	
-do-	25th		The Battalion holding Support Line. Working parties on new Front Line and under R.E.'s furnished. On this date LIEUT-COLONEL J.H.BRIDCUTT.D.S.O. joined the Battalion, this Officer took over command of the Battalion from MAJOR H.CLENDINING.	

VOL. 6. Sheet 3.

WAR DIARY of 2nd BN: THE ROYAL IRISH RIFLES.
(Erase heading not required.)

Army Form C. 2118.

AUGUST 1918

Map Refs:- (See p.p.1)

Place	Date	Hour	Summary of Events and Information	Remarks and references to Appendices
LA MANCHE COPSE	26th		The Battalion holding Support Line in 107th Infantry Brigade Sector. Working parties supplied for R.E's on strengthening positions and rebuilding dug-outs etc.	
P.32.b. central	27th		Battalion holding Support Line as above. On this night the Battalion was relieved and proceeded to Training Area at about P.32.b.central. Dispositions were as follows :- "A" Company 19d "B" Coy 25b "C" Coy. about 26a "D" Coy. at 31d.	
-do-	28th		Battalion in Billets. This day was devoted to general cleaning up and Arms, Kit, Respirator Inspections. etc etc. Captain A.E.KEMP took over command and payment of "C" Company from Lieut.A.E.Buttle, this Officer having previously taken over command of that Company from LIEUT.T.N.INGLIS who had left the Battalion to join the G.H.Q. Supernumerary Wireless Dept. Captain L.G.de R.BARCLAY joined the Battalion on this date and took over command and payment of "C" Company from Captain A.E.KEMP, D.C.M.	
-do-	29th		Battalion in Billets. Two Companies were able to get bathed on this day in Improvised Baths erected in one of the Coys. Billets. The Service Dress of the men was also disinfected at the Baths.	
-do-	30th		Battalion in Billets. A party of 87 Other Ranks, including a draft of 17 Other Ranks joined the Battalion on this date. The following Officers also joined the Battalion:- Captain G.B.J.SMYTH and 2nd LIEUT.E.R.MORGAN. Bathing as yesterday was continued. Re-organisation and refitting was also speedily carried out.	
-do-	31st		Battalion in Billets. Commanding Officer inspected the Battalion by Companies in Service Order in the forenoon. On this date news was received that the enemy had fallen back on the BAILLEUL Front and the Battalion was ordered to proceed to the MONT NOIR and MONT KOKEREELE Area where it arrived at about 7 p.m. and took up a position in Reserve to the 109th Infantry Brigade.	

-- F I N I S --

1.9.1918.

LIEUT-COLONEL
COMMANDING, 2nd BATTALION, THE ROYAL IRISH RIFLES.

Volume VII
Sheet I

WAR DIARY

~~INTELLIGENCE SUMMARY~~

2nd BN. THE ROYAL IRISH RIFLES.

(Erase heading not required.)

SEPTEMBER 1918

Army Form C. 2118.

Reference Maps:-
Sheet 28 N.W. Sheet 28 S.W.
Sheet 28 N.E. Sheet 27 S.E. and 28 S.W.
Berthen and Meteren. Hazebrouck 5 a
GHELUVELT.

Place	Date	Hour	Summary of Events and Information	Remarks and references to Appendices
S.11.d.	1st		On this date the Battalion proceeded from Reserve Billets at WOLFHOEK to CYPRIAN FARM at S.11.c. passing CROIX DE POPERINGHE at 8-25 p.m. and relieved the 1st Bn. Royal Irish Fusrs. Battalion Headquarters was established at S.11.c.60.40.	
-do-	2nd		The Battalion was located in above position and awaited orders to move forward.	
-do-	3rd		The Battalion moved forward to area T.8.c. T.14.a. T.7.d. T.13.b.	
T.8.c. -do-	4th		The Battalion remained in Brigade Support in above area.	
-do-	5th		During this day Battalion remained in Support Line but on night 5/6th inst proceeded to the front line relieving 9th Royal Irish Fusiliers (109th Infantry Brigade).	
T.6.c.6.5.	6th		On this date, the Battalion assisted by one company of the 1st Royal Irish Rifles carried out an operation. Report of operations as follows:- "By 3-30 p.m. 6th September,1918 half an hour before ZERO the troops were in position. Three Companies in the Firing Line:- "A" "B" "C" 2nd R.I.Rifles. Twon Companies in Support:- "D" Company 1st R.I.Rifles. "D" Company 2nd R.I.Rifles. these twon companies were concealed behind bushes on or near the jumping off line. At schedule time the guns opened and troops that were not exactly in their places moved from their concealment to get there ready to advance when the barrage lifted. According to time table the barrage lifted and the troops advanced in small wormlike columns picking their way through the undergrowth and uncut wire moving steadily forward until their objectives were reached when Battle Outposts were pushed forward as near as possible to the standing barrage line, the troops consolidating HANBURY SUPPORT TRENCH. When darkness came on Patrols were pushed forward to gain touch with the Bosche - He was found to be holding a piece of trench in the trench system U.d.central at the same time a considerable amount of M.G.fire was coming from the direction of:- (a) The Crater in U.I.a. (b) Mortar Farm in M.36.d. (c) Trench system T.6.b.	

(1)

Volume VII
Sheet x 2

WAR DIARY
INTELLIGENCE SUMMARY.

SEPTEMBER 1918

Army Form C. 2118.

Instructions regarding War Diaries and Intelligence Summaries are contained in F. S. Regs., Part II. and the Staff Manual respectively. Title pages will be prepared in manuscript.

(Erase heading not required.)

Place	Date	Hour	Summary of Events and Information	Remarks and references to Appendices
T.6.c.6.5.	6th		For reference maps:- See page 1. A good deal of the latter was taking the men in rear and naturally they began to think the Bosche was surrounding them - to counter-act this I ordered my left supporting Company ("D" Company 1st R.I.Rifles) to form a defensive flank between the support and front line - this was done in a very efficient manner by Captain P.J.CULLEN. The objectives were all taken except GABION FARM some little delay was experienced in establishing a post here as it was difficult to tell or recognise the exact spot but inside 1 hour this had been done and the post put out and handed over on relief. On the left flank BOWLES FARM and CRATER was given as an objective - this was taken but on examination of the ground the Company Commander on the spot decided it would be very much better to hold the trench system which runs some 30 to 40 yards west of these two places - I personally examined this by daylight and could not help but support his opinion and agreed to his action on the grounds that his men were being very badly shot at from the left rear chiefly from the trenches in T.6.b. also that BOYLES FARM was denied the BOSCHE. Casualties:- Officers Killed 2 Wounded 2 Other Ranks Killed:- 18 Wounded:- 148	
-do-	7th		The Battalion holding newly captured Line as above. As the enemy shewed no signs of counter-attack the Company of the 1st Royal Irish Rifles withdrew to their own Battalion Companies of this Battalion were then arranged as follows:- "A" Company holding Right Front Line "B" Company holding Left Front Line. "C" Company in Left Support and "D" Company in KING EDWARD TRENCH (Right Support).	
-do- and NEUVE EGLISE	8th		The Battalion was relieved from the front Line and proceeded to Reserve to NEUVE EGLISE.	
-do-	9th		The Battalion in Reserve Billets in NEUVE EGLISE.	
-do-	10th		The Battalion in Reserve Billets in NEUVE EGLISE.	
-do-	11th		The Battalion in Reserve Billets in NEUVE EGLISE.	
-do-	12th		During this day Battalion found working parties for New Brigade Headquarters. On night 12/13th the Battalion proceeded to relieve the 15th (S) Battalion, THE ROYAL IRISH RIFLES in Support Line.	
SUPPORT LINE				

Volume VII
Sheet 2

WAR DIARY
~~INTELLIGENCE SUMMARY~~

SEPTEMBER 1918

Army Form C. 2118.

Instructions regarding War Diaries and Intelligence Summaries are contained in F. S. Regs., Part II. and the Staff Manual respectively. Title pages will be prepared in manuscript.

(Erase heading not required.)

Place	Date	Hour	For map references See Sheet 1 — Summary of Events and Information	Remarks and references to Appendices
SUPPORT LINE	13th		The Battalion holding Support Line. Working parties engaged on erection of new Brigade Headquarters and New Support Battalion Headquarters also parties were furnished for carrying material for this task.	
-do-	14th		The Battalion holding Support Line as above. The Battalion was engaged on Carrying work. Trench Mortars and Bombs were carried to the Front Line. Work was also done by our men in the Front Line on this date.	
-do-	15th		The Battalion was holding Support Line as above. The same working parties were found. On the night of 15th/16th the Battalion was relieved by the 1st Royal Innis.Fusiliers and proceeded to Billets in the PIEBROUCK-ROSSIGNOL AREA. Battalion Headquarters was at R.27.a.10.90. Half-way on the route from the trenches to Billets a hot meal was serevd up to the men.	
R.27.a.10.90.	16th		The Battalion in Billets in the PIEBROUCK - ROSSIGNOL AREA. The day was devoted to cleaning up etc etc.	
-do-	17th		The Battalion in Billets as above. Commanding Officer's inspection. Cleaning of Kit, Arms etc continued - Baths at PIEBROUCK utilized. Re-fitting of clothing. Re-organisation of Companies carried out.	
-do-	18th		The Battalion in Billets in above area. Draft of 139 Other Ranks joined the Battalion on this date.	
-do-	19th		On this date the Battalion moved to the St SYLVESTRE CAPEL AREA. by march route, by way of Cross country tracks West of Square R.19 then by main road starting at 11-30 a.m. and arriving in new billets at 2-15 p.m. On this date the Division joined the II Corps.	
Q.13.b.4.9. -do-	20th		On this date the Battalion proceeded by march route to ESQUELBECQ. Tea was served at a ½ hour halt en route.	

(2)

Volume VII
Sheet 4

WAR DIARY

~~INTELLIGENCE~~ SUMMARY

Army Form C. 2118.

SEPTEMBER 1918

(Erase heading not required.)

For map reference:-
See Sheet 1.

Place	Date	Hour	Summary of Events and Information	Remarks and references to Appendices
ESQUELBECQ	21st		The Battalion arrived in ESQUELBECQ at about 1 a.m. Battalion Headquarters was at Sheet 27 B.&.b.8.1. Remainder of day was devoted to rest and cleaning of Kit, arms, etc. etc.	
-do-	22nd		The Battalion was billetted in ESQUELBECQ. Sunday - No training was carried out. Battalion attended Divine Services according to denominations. Companies were billetted as follows:- "A" Company at B.12.b.7.7. "B" Company at C.8.a.7.1. "C" Company at C.8.a.7.1. "D" Company at C.7.a.0.6.	
-do-	23rd		The Battalion billetted in ESQUELBECQ. On this date the Commanding Officer inspected the Platoons of each Company carry out a Platoon attack practice on a selected piece of ground.	
-do-	24th		The Battalion billetted in ESQUELBECQ. The G.O.C.Division on this date presented Medal Ribbons to Warrant Officers, N.C.O's and men of the Battalion who had been awarded Medals but who had not been officially presented with same. After the parade the Battalion marched past the G.O.C.	
-do-	25th		The Battalion was billetted in ESQUE:BECQ. At 9-30 a.m. the Battalion paraded with the Transport and proceeded for a short route march returning to Billets at 11-30 a.m. On this date orders had been received to be prepared to move at short notice and the remainder of the day was devoted in making preparations for this emergency.	
-do-	26th		The Battalion, on this date, proceeded by march route from ESQUELBECQ to TUNNELLERS CAMP. (PROVEN AREA) where it remained for the night and part of the following day. In the morning a previously selected party of Officers N.C.O's and men forming the Battalion's Surplus Personnel proceeded to join the 36th Divisional Reception Camp.	

Volume VII
Sheet c5

WAR DIARY
~~INTELLIGENCE SUMMARY~~
(Erase heading not required.)

Army Form C. 2118.

SEPTEMBER 1918

Instructions regarding War Diaries and Intelligence Summaries are contained in F. S. Regs., Part II. and the Staff Manual respectively. Title pages will be prepared in manuscript.

Place	Date	Hour	Summary of Events and Information (For map reference:- See Sheet L)	Remarks and references to Appendices
TUNNELLERS CAMP	27th		The Battalion was billetted in TUNNELLERS CAMP. Orders were received that the Brigade would be moving that evening to Area "P" "F" and "X" Camps and preliminary arrangements were completed. On this date the Commanding Officer paraded those N.C.O's and men who had received Medals for the Operation on the 6th and congratulated them on their awards. MAJOR H.CLENDINING left the Battalion on this date for ENGLAND on Leave prior to joining Senior Officers School at ALDERSHOT. Battalion moved at dusk to "P" and "X" Camps.	
"P" AND "F" CAMPS.	-do- 28th		Battalion arrived at "P" and "X" Camps. On this date Greatcoats were rolled and all surplus Kits dumped under arrangements made by 107th Infantry Brigade in "P" Camp. Other preliminary arrangements, prior to going into action, were carried out. Bombs etc were drawn. At 5 p.m. the Battalion entrained at BYNG SIDING in "P" Camp Area and proceeded by Light Railway Train to vicinity of HELL FIRE CORNER East of YPRES where the Battalion remained in an open Field for the remainder of the night, where it was subjected to fire from hostile aircraft. There were no casualties except 1 horse slightly wounded.	
I.10.c.	29th		On this date at 7 a.m. the Battalion proceeded by march route to WESTHOEK RIDGE where it remained in various Pill Boxes, trenches etc.	
BECELAERE	30th		At 4-50 a.m. on this date the Battalion proceeded to BECELAIRE AREA.	
			TOTAL CASUALTIES:- 2nd LIEUT.W.EATON. KILLED IN ACTION. LIEUT.V.C.YOUNG. WOUNDED IN ACTION LIEUT.H.D.MITCHESS. W.I.A. LIEUT.H.CUMMING. WOUNDED IN ACTION. LIEUT.W.F.HUNTER. WOUNDED IN ACTION. Other Ranks:- 28 Wounded:- 280 Missing 10.	

OCTOBER 1st 1918.

MAJOR.,
Commanding, 2nd BATTALION, THE ROYAL IRISH RIFLES.

Volume I
Sheet I

WAR DIARY
~~INTELLIGENCE SUMMARY~~
2nd BN: THE ROYAL IRISH RIFLES.
(Erase heading not required.)

Army Form C. 2118.

10/36
October 18
vol 47

Instructions regarding War Diaries and Intelligence Summaries are contained in F.S. Regs., Part II. and the Staff Manual respectively. Title pages will be prepared in manuscript.

Reference Maps:-
Sheet 28 N.E. 3 & 4   Sheet 29.

Place	Date	Hour	Summary of Events and Information	Remarks and references to Appendices
West of TERHAND	1st		The Battalion attacked at dawn., "A" and "C" Companies passing through "D" and "B" Companies - but was unable to make any advance on account of Machine Gun Fire from CLARBROUGH HOUSE and WHEATLEY CORNER. Lieut-Colonel J.H. BRIDCUTT. D.S.O. was Killed 150 yds North of CARLTON HOUSE. The Battalion was then taken over by Captain G.B.J. SMYTH and was relieved by the 1st Battn. The Royal Irish Rifles when it marched to TERHAND into Brigade Reserve where Major J.D. McCALLUM. D.S.O. (15th Royal Irish Rifles) took command. The Battalion suffered about 183 Casualties.	
TERHAND	2nd	)	The Battalion remained in Area North of TERHAND in Brigade Reserve.	
TERHAND	3rd	)	At dusk the Battalion moved into Brigade Support - S.E. of TERHAND.	
TERHAND	4th	)	Battalion Headquarters being entrenched N. of CACKLE COPSE.	
CACKLE COPSE	5th		At 2300 the Battalion was relieved by the 105th Infantry Brigade, 35th Division and marched to Area of REUTEL - West of BECELAERE where it remained in Tents and bivouacs.	
REUTEL	6th		The day spent in Resting and cleaning and settling down in new area.	
REUTEL	7th		Company Inspections and re-fitting of Battalion. Lieut-Colonel C.M.L. BECHER. D.S.O., took command of the Battalion.	
REUTEL	8th		Company Inspections and re-fitting of Battalion.	
REUTEL	9th		Company Inspections and re-fitting of Battalion.	
REUTEL	10th		Captain R. WATTS. M.C. was appointed Adjutant of the Battalion.	
REUTEL	11th		Training under Company arrangements, etc, etc.	
REUTEL	12th		Training carried out under Company arrangements as for yesterday.	

(1)

Volume I
Sheet 2

WAR DIARY
of
~~INTELLIGENCE SUMMARY~~.
(Erase heading not required.)

Army Form C. 2118.

OCTOBER, 1918

Place	Date	Hour	Map References:- See p.p. 1. Summary of Events and Information	Remarks and references to Appendices
REUTEL	13th		The Battalion was moved from the REUTEL AREA at 2030. Order of march :- H.Q.F. - "A" - "C" - "B" and "D" Companies and proceeded to the Assembly Position at J.16.d. On arrival Battalion Headquarters was established at ROBERTSON HOUSE for the night.	
J.16.d.	14th		At 0535 the Battalion, in Brigade Reserve taking part in the General Attack advanced through a thick Mist in Artillery formation, - "A" Company on the right with "B" Company in Support "C" Company on the left with "D" Company in Support, passing through the 15th Royal Irish Rifles at MOORSEELE they came into Brigade Support and advanced to a Line running N and S to the West of GULLEGHEM. Battalion Headquarters being at Sheet 29, G.19.a.8.1. At 2000. Battalion Headquarters were established at Sheet 28. L.24.a.45.80. South of BARLEY CORNER.	
L.24.a. 45.80.	15th		At 0900 the attack was resumed and the Battalion advanced in Brigade Support to the Grid Line running N and S through G.22.central. Battalion Headquarters were established at Sheet 29 G.21.c.7.7. At 1530 the Battalion passed through the 1st Bn.Royal Irish Rifles and resumed the attack capturing HEULE and the Corps First Objective from G.24.a.8.5. to Road at G.24.a.3.7. A patrol under 2nd Lieut.C.RULE. "C" Coy. which was sent out entered COURTRAI and found that all Bridges crossing the LYS RIVER had been destroyed.	
G.23.c.	16th		At 0530 the 108th Infantry Brigade passed through the Battalion and resumed the advance. At 1430 the Battalion less "C" Company withdrew to Area round Sheet 28 F.27.a. "C" Company remained at HEULE - Sh.29, G.24.a.1.5. to collect salvage, etc.	
F.27.a.	17th		Day spent in Cleaning and resting.	
F.27.a.	18th		"C" Company rejoined the Battalion at 0900. At 1030 the Battalion was addressed by the BG.C. 107th Infantry Brigade and afterwards marched past. At 1400 the Battalion left Area Sheet 28, F.27.a. and marched to LENDELEDE AREA. Battalion Headquarters were established at Sheet 29 B.19.c.4.3.	
B.19.c.	19th		Day spent in refitting.	

Volume I
Sheet 3.

WAR DIARY of INTELLIGENCE SUMMARY.
2nd BN: THE ROYAL IRISH RIFLES.
OCTOBER, 1918

Army Form C. 2118.

Instructions regarding War Diaries and Intelligence Summaries are contained in F. S. Regs., Part II. and the Staff Manual respectively. Title pages will be prepared in manuscript.

(Erase heading not required.)

Place	Date	Hour	Summary of Events and Information	Remarks and references to Appendices
			Map references:- See p.p.1.	
B.19.c.	20th		The Battalion left LENDELEDE at 0545 and marched to Ammunition Dump at Sh.29. B.17.d.9.1. at 0600 the Battalion advanced in Brigade Reserve with the General Attack.	
B.19.c.	21st		The Battalion was in Support in Area 19.c.10. (less 1 Company) who were East of this and under command of the 1st Bn. The Royal Irish Rifles.	
19c.10.	22nd		At 0900 the Battalion attacked with 3 Companies in the Line and 1 in Support from a Line running between Sheet 29 I.18.b.8.9. and Sheet 29, I.18.b.2.6. and advanced to a Line running from Sheet 29, J.26.a.6.1. to WINDMILL at Sh.29 J.20.c.4.9. to Sh.29. J.19.b.9.9. One Company of 15th Royal Irish Rifles was attached to the Battalion and was in Brigade Reserve. Battalion Headquarters were at Sh.29. I.17.d.99.29.	
I.17.d.	23rd		The Battalion was relieved by a Unit of the 108th Infantry Brigade at dusk and withdrew to BAVICHOVE. Battalion Headquarters were at Sh. 19. B24.a.3.3.	
B.24.a	24th		Cleaning up and re-fitting.	
B.24.a.	25th		The Battalion moved at 1930 to Area. Sh.29. I.28 and 29. Battalion Headquarters at Sh.29. I.29.a.5.7.	
I29.a.	26th		At 1410 the Battalion moved back to LENDELEDE and occupied old Billets. Battalion Headquarters being at Sh.19. B19.c.4.3.	
B.19.c.	27th		Battalion left LENDELEDE at 0940 and marched to Sh.29. N.29.and 35. Battalion Headquarters were at Sh. 29. N.35.a.8.4. A halt for dinners was made near MARCKE.	
N.35.a.	28th		Resting and cleaning.	
N.35.a.	29th		Training under Company arrangements etc etc.	
N.35.a.	30th		Training under Company arrangements etcetc.	
N.35.a.	31st		Ditto.	

Volume I
Sheet IV

WAR DIARY

2nd BN. THE ROYAL IRISH RIFLES.

OCTOBER, 1918

Army Form C. 2118.

Instructions regarding War Diaries and Intelligence Summaries are contained in F. S. Regs., Part II. and the Staff Manual respectively. Title pages will be prepared in manuscript.

Place	Date	Hour	Summary of Events and Information	Remarks and references to Appendices
			The following casualties amongst Officers occurred during the month:-	
			LIEUT-COLONEL J.H.BRIDCUTT. D.S.O. KILLED IN ACTION	
			CAPTAIN A.E.KEMP. D.C.M. WOUNDED IN ACTION.	
			LIEUT. A.E.BUTTLE. WOUNDED IN ACTION. (since D.O.W.)	
			LIEUT. F.K.McKEEMAN. WOUNDED IN ACTION.	
			The following Officers joined the Battalion during the month:-	
			LIEUT-COL. C.N.L.BECHER. D.S.O.	
			MAJOR C.W.GARNER. LIEUT.T.C.WALLIS.M.C. 2nd LT.J.CRAWFORD.	
			LIEUT.D.O.C.BEALE. CAPT.W.SOMERS.M.C.	
			2nd LIEUT.J.K.WATSON. LIEUT.R.D.WILLIAMS. M.C.	
			2nd LIEUT.J.R.FORBES. LIEUT.J.W.McGHIE.	
			2nd LIEUT.G.H.ADAMS. 2nd LIEUT.W.R.SLOANE.	
			2nd LIEUT.T.R.BOND. 2nd LIEUT.T.E.BRYANS.	
	1/11/1918.		C.W.Garner Major for LIEUT-COLONEL. COMMANDING., 2nd BATTALION, THE ROYAL IRISH RIFLES.	

Volume I
Sheet 1.

WAR DIARY
of
~~XXXXXXXXXXXXXXXXXXXXXXXXXX~~
2nd BATTN. ROYAL IRISH RIFLES.

NOVEMBER, 1918.

Army Form C. 2118.

Instructions regarding War Diaries and Intelligence Summaries are contained in F. S. Regs., Part II. and the Staff Manual respectively. Title pages will be prepared in manuscript.

Reference Maps.
Sheets 28 and 29.   Tourcoing.

Place	Date	Hour	Summary of Events and Information	Remarks and references to Appendices
RECKEM	1st	1420	The Battalion moved from the Area at 29 N.35.a. to RECKEM where Battalion Headquarters was established in 28. R.29.a.7.9. Companies who had gone to Baths in the morning at St ANNE 29. N.19.a.1.4. did not march with the Battalion but proceeded direct to their new area.	
-do-	2nd		Parades under Company arrangements during the morning.	
MOUSCRON.	3rd		At 0917 the Battalion moved to the MOUSCRON Area. Battalion Headquarters were established at 29 S.16.a.3.0.	
-do-	4th		Battalion carried out Training in vicinity of Billets.	
-do-	5th		Battalion carried out Training in vicinity of Billets.	
-do-	6th		Battalion carried out Training in vicinity of Billets.	
-do-	7th		Battalion carried out Training in vicinity of Billets.	
-do-	8th		The Battalion went for a Route March during the morning.	
-do-	9th		Sunday - Divine Services held during the morning. In the afternoon the Battalion took part in the 107th Infantry Brigade Sports.	
-do-	10th		Training under Company arrangements. On this date Captain R.O. MANSERGH rejoined the Battalion and resumed command of "D" Company.	

(1).

Vol. I.
Sheet 11.

WAR DIARY

2nd BATTN: ROYAL IRISH RIFLES.

NOVEMBER, 1918.

Army Form C. 2118.

Instructions regarding War Diaries and Intelligence Summaries are contained in F. S. Regs., Part II. and the Staff Manual respectively. Title pages will be prepared in manuscript.

Place	Date	Hour	Summary of Events and Information	Remarks and references to Appendices
			Ref; Maps See p.p. 1.	
MOUSCRON.	11th	X	During the morning the Battalion carried out a Rehearsal parade prior to the Divisional Commander's Inspection.	
-do-	12th		The Battalion attended a Brigade Rehearsal for the Inspection of the Divisional Commanders Inspection.	
-do-	13th		The Battalion attended the inspection of the 107th Infantry Brigade by the Divisional Commander. The following Officers were presented with Military Cross Ribbons:- Captain W.B.TEELE.M.C. and 2nd Lieut. J.McH.WRIGHT.M.C. Notification was received on this date that the following Officers had been awarded the Military Cross:- Captain A.E.KEMP. D.C.M. and 2nd Lieut. F.ADAMS.	
-do-	14th		The Battalion took part in a Brigade Route march.	
-do-	15th		The Battalion carried out Training under Company arrangements,	
-do-	16th		The Commanding Officer inspected the Battalion's Billets and later on addressed the Battalion in the morning.	
-do-	17th		A Thanksgiving Service was held in the CASINO PALACE, ROUBAIX to which the Battalion sent representatives and afterwards marches past the Acting Army Commander, Lieut-General Claude JACOB, K.C.B.	
-do-	18th		The Battalion carried out Musketry practices and Training under Company arrangements.	

Volume 1.
Sheet 3.

WAR DIARY
of
2nd BATTN: ROYAL IRISH RIFLES.

NOVEMBER, 1918.

Army Form C. 2118.

Reference Maps:- See p.p. 1.

Place	Date	Hour	Summary of Events and Information	Remarks and references to Appendices
MOUSCRON.	19th		The Battalion carried out Training under Company arrangements.	
-do-	20th		The Battalion took part in a Brigade Concentration march.	
-do-	21st		The Battalion carried out Training in vicinity of Billets.	
-do-	22nd		The Battalion took part in the 107th Infantry Brigade Advance Guard Scheme.	
-do-	23rd		The Battalion carried out Training in vicinity of Billets.	
-do-	24th		The Battalion carried out Training in vicinity of Billets. On this date Captain R.H.LORIE joined the Battalion and took over command of "C" Company.	
-do-	25th		The Battalion carried out Training in vicinity of Billets.	
-do-	26th		The Battalion took part in a Brigade Advance Guard Scheme. Lieut.R.F.Patterson joined the Battalion on this date.	
-do-	27th		The Battalion carried out Training in vicinity of Billets.	
-do-m	28th		The Battalion carried out Training in vicinity of Billets.	
-do-	29th		The Battalion carried outv Training in vicinity of Billets.	
-do-	30th		The Battalion took part in an Advance Guard Scheme.	

----------o0o----------

1/12/1918.

MAJOR.,
Commanding, 2nd BATTALION, ROYAL IRISH RIFLES.

Volume I
Sheet I

Army Form C. 2118.

WAR DIARY
of
~~INTELLIGENCE SUMMARY~~
2nd BATTALION, ROYAL IRISH RIFLES.

DECEMBER, 1918.

Place	Date	Hour	Summary of Events and Information	Remarks and references to Appendices
			Reference Sheets:- 28, 29 and 37. Tournai 5.	
MOUSCRON	1st		The Battalion was billetted in MOUSCRON. The Battalion attended Divine Services during the morning.	
"	2nd		The Battalion took part in Ceremonial rehearsal parade for Corps Commender's Inspection at a later date. Battalion paraded for above rehearsal on Ground at 4.C.3.9. (Tournai 5).	
"	3rd		Capt. R. WATTS. MC; rejoined the Battalion on this date and resumed duties of Adjutant. The Battalion carried out a Route March.	
"	4th		The Battalion carried out Training in vicinity of Billets.	
"	5th		The Battalion carried out Military, Educational and Recreational Training in vicinity of Billets.	
"	6th		The Battalion took part in Divisional practice Ceremonial parade at HALLUIN AERODROME	
"	7th		The Battalion carried out Training as on December 5th, 1918. A party of 1 Officer and 135 Other Ranks marched to ROUBAIX as HIS MAJESTY THE KING was passing through the Town.	
"	8th		Sunday - Divine Services held for all denominations.	
"	9th		The Battalion carried out Military, Educational and Recreational Training in vicintiy of Billets. Notification was received on this date that the following Officers and men had been awarded the Decorations stated:-	

French Croix de Guerre a l'ordre Division.　　　French Croix de Guerre a l'order Brigade

Captain R. Watts. M.C.　　　　　　　　　　　　Lieutenant A. M. Anderson.
47356 Rifleman P. McCABE. DCM.　　　　　　　　2/Lieut. C. Rule.

(1)

Volume I
Sheet II

Army Form C. 2118.

WAR DIARY
of
2nd BATTALION, ROYAL IRISH RIFLES.

DECEMBER, 1918.

Place	Date	Hour	Summary of Events and Information	Remarks and references to Appendices
			For Reference Sheets See pp. I.	
MOUSCRON.	10th		The Battalion carried out Training in vicinity of Billets.	
"	11th		The Battalion carried out Training in vicinity of Billets.	
"	12th		The Battalion carried out Training in vicinity of Billets.	
"	13th		The Battalion carried out a Route March during the morning.	
"	14th		The Battalion carried out Training in vicinity of Billets.	
"	15th		Sunday - Divine Services held for all denominations.	
"	16th		The Battalion took part in a Divisional Parade and were inspected by the CORPS COMMENDER at HALLUIN AERODROME.	
"	17th		The Battalion carried out Training in vicinity of Billets. Captain W. SOMERS, M.C. was struck off the strength of the Battalion on being appointed 107th Infantry Brigade Intelligence Officer.	
"	18th		The Battalion carried out Training in vicinity of Billets.	
"	19th		The Battalion carried out Training in vicinity of Billets.	
"	20th		The Battalion carried out Training in the vicinity of Billets.	
"	21st		The Brigadier General Commanding inspected the Billets occupied by the Battalion.	
"	22nd		Sunday - Divine Services held for all Denominations.	
"	23rd		The Battalion carried out Military, Educational and Recreational Training in vicinity of Billets.	

Volume I
Sheet III

WAR DIARY
of
~~INTELLIGENCE SUMMARY~~
2nd BATTALION, ROYAL IRISH RIFLES.

DECEMBER, 1918.

Army Form C. 2118.

Place	Date	Hour	Summary of Events and Information	Remarks and references to Appendices
MOUSCRON.	24th		The Battalion carried out an hour's Physical Training and returned to Billets for the purpose of cleaning equipment. There was a Midnight Mass Service on this date for Roman Catholics in the St Charles LUINGNE Convent.	
"	25th		CHRISTMAS DAY. During the morning Divine Services were held for all Denominations.	
"	26th		BOXING DAY. A Check parade was carried out during the morning.	
"	27th		The Battalion carried out a Route March from 09.00 to 12.30 hours but after the Battalion had been on the road for about an hour had to return to Billets owing to the inclement weather. Training was carried on in Company Billets.	
"	28th		Battalion proceeded to Divisional Baths and was afterwards inspected by the Medical Officer.	
"	29th		Sunday - Divine Services held for all Denominations.	
"	30th		The Battalion carried out Military, Educational, and Recreational Training in vicinity of Billets.	
"	31st		The Battalion carried out same Training as for 30th instant in vicinity of Billets.	

JANUARY 1st 1919.

C Becher
LIEUT-COLONEL.,
Commanding, 2nd BATTALION, ROYAL IRISH RIFLES.

Volume 1.
Sheet 1.

WAR DIARY
2nd BATTALION ROYAL IRISH RIFLES.

JANUARY 1919

Army Form C. 2118

Reference Maps.
Sheets:- 28 - 29 - 37 TOURNAI 5

Place	Date	Hour	Summary of Events and Information	Remarks and references to Appendices
MOUSCRON	1st.		During the Month of December 18 Other Ranks were sent to United Kingdom to be demobilized. The Battalion was billeted in the town of MOUSCRON near TOURCOING and ROUBAIX. The Battalion attended Divine Service in the morning. During the afternoon the Battalion used the Divisional Baths. Four Other Ranks were sent to United Kingdom to be demobilized.	
"	2nd		One Other Rank sent to U.K. to be demobilized. The Battalion carried out a Route March from 09.00 to 12.30 hours in full marching order.	
"	3rd.		Educational, recreational and military Training carried out in vicinity of Company billets. Football Match in the afternoon.	
"	4th		Two Other Ranks to U.K. to be demobilized. Billet and Kit Inspection carried out by Company Officers from 09.00 to 11.00 hours. At 11.00 hours the Commanding Officer inspected the billets, at which time all kits were laid for inspection. Educational Classes were cancelled on this day.	
"	5th		Sunday - Divine Services were held for all Denominations.	
"	6th		Educational Recreational and Miliatry Training carried out in vicinity of Company billets. 107th and 109th Brigade Rugby Match at RONCQ, in the afternoon.	
"	7th		Three Other Ranks sent to U.K. to be demobilized. Educational, Recreational and Military Training carried out in vicinity of Company billets	
"	8th			

Volume 1
Sheet 11.

WAR DIARY

2nd BATTALION, ROYAL IRISH RIFLES.

JANUARY 1919.

Army Form C. 2118.

Place	Date	Hour	References Maps. Sheets (see page 1)	Summary of Events and Information	Remarks and references to Appendices
MOUSCRON	8th			Educational, Recreational and Military Training carried out in the vicinity of Company billets in the morning. In the afternoon the Battalion used the Divisional Baths and all blankets were fumigated.	
"	9th			Educational Recreational and Military Training carried out in vicinity of Company billets	
"	10th			Physical Drill and Training carried out in vicinity of Company billets from 09.00 to 10.00 hours. At 11.00 hours the Battalion proceeded for a Route March.	
"	11th			10 Other Ranks sent to U.K. to be demobilized. Information received that Major H. Glendening had been awarded the D.S.O. and No. 4115 Rifleman Gillman M.M. the D.C.M. Training carried out in vicinity of Company billets.	
"	12th			Sunday - Divine Services held for all Denominations. 11 Other Ranks sent to U.K. for Demobilization.	
"	13th			8 Other Ranks sent to U.K. to be Demobilized. Educational, Recreational and Military Training carried out in vicinity of Company billets	
"	14th			Educational, Recreational and Military Training carried out in vicinity of Company billets	
"	15th			Educational, Recreational and Military Training carried out in vicinity of Company billets	
"	16th			Educational, Recreational and Military Training carried out in vicinity of Company billets also Medical Inspection.	

Volume 1
Sheet 111.

WAR DIARY
or
INTELLIGENCE SUMMARY.
2nd BATTALION, ROYAL IRISH RIFLES.

Army Form C. 2118.

JANUARY 1919

Place	Date	Hour	References Map, Sheets (See 1st sheet)	Summary of Events and Information	Remarks and references to Appendices
MOUSCRON	17th			Educational, Recreational and Military Training carried out in vicinity of Company billets	
"	18th			Lecture by the A.D.M.S. 36th Division in hall at St. Joseph's College MOUSCRON on the "Dangers of Venereal Disease" after lecture Physical Traing and Drill was carried out in vicinity of Company Billets.	
"	19th			Sunday - Divine Services held for all Denominations. One Other Rank sent to U.K. for Demobilization.	
"	20th			Educational, Recreational and Military Training carried out in vicinity of company billets	
"	21st.			2 Other Ranks sent to U.K. to be Demobilized. Educational, Recreational and Military Training carried out in vicinity of company billets.	
"	22nd			5 Other Ranks sent to U.K. to be Demobilized. Educational, Recreational and Military Training carried out in vicinity of Company billets. In the Afternoon the Battalion used the Divisional Baths and all Blankets were fumigated.	
"	23rd.			Educational, Recreational and Military Training carried out in vicinity of Company billets Lewis Guns and Rifles were inspected by the Army Inspector.	
"	24th			Educational, Recreational and Military Training carried out in vicinity of Company Billets Rifles inspected by Army Inspector.	
"	25th			3 Other Ranks sent to U.K. to be demobilized. Educational, Recreational and Military Training carried out in vicinity of Company billets also Medical inspection.	

Volume 1.
Sheet 1V.

WAR DIARY

2nd BATTALION, ROYAL IRISH RIFLES.

JANUARY. 1919.

Army Form C. 2118.

Place	Date	Hour	References Map Sheets (See sheet 1) Summary of Events and Information	Remarks and references to Appendices
MOUSCRON.	26th		2 Other Ranks sent to U.K. to be demobilized. Sunday - Divine Services were held for all Denominations.	
"	27th		27 Other Ranks sent to U. K. to be demobilized. Educational, Recreational and Military Training carried out in vicinity of Company billets.	
"	28th		7 Other Ranks sent to U. K. to be Demobilized. Educational, Recreational and Military Training carried out in vicinity of Company billets.	
"	29th		6 Other Ranks sent to U. K. to be demobilized. Educational, Recreational and Military Training carried out in vicinity of Company billets. The Battalion used the Divisional Baths in the afternoon and all blankets were fumigated.	
"	30th		Educational, Recreational and Military Training carried out in vicinity of Company billets.	
"	31st.		Educational, Recreational and Military Training carried out in vicinity of Company billets.	
			Total number of men Demobilized during the Month of January - 92.	

C Becher.
LIEUT-COLONEL.
Commanding, 2nd BATTALION, ROYAL IRISH RIFLES.

1st. FEBRUARY 1919.

Volume I
Sheet I

WAR DIARY
of
~~INTELLIGENCE HEADQUARTERS SUMMARY~~
2nd BATTALION, ROYAL IRISH RIFLES.
(Erase heading not required.)

February -1919-

Army Form C. 2118.

Instructions regarding War Diaries and Intelligence Summaries are contained in F. S. Regs., Part II, and the Staff Manual respectively. Title pages will be prepared in manuscript.

Reference Maps:- Sheets 28, 29 and 37.

vol 51

Place	Date	Hour	Summary of Events and Information	Remarks and references to Appendices
MOUSCRON	1st		The Battalion was billetted in the town of MOUSCRON. On this date H.R.H. The Prince of Wales visited the Battalion. Educational Classes, Recreational and Physical Training were carried on during the morning.	
-do-	2nd		Sunday - Divine Services held for all denominations. Sixteen Other Ranks sent to England for demobilization.	
-do-	3rd		Military, Educational and Recreational Training carried out during the morning according to Weekly Training Programme. Eighteen Other Ranks despatched to ENGLAND for demobilization.	
-do-	4th		Usual Training carried out. Lecture to men by the Medical Officer at 12.00 hours on the "Dangers of Venereal Disease". On this date A 'Bus service to LILLE was commenced for the benefit of Officers and men billetted in MOUSCRON desirous of visiting the City of LILLE.	
-do-	5th		Training carried out in the vicinity of Company Billets. Lecture by Medical Officer. Seven Other Ranks proceeded to ENGLAND for demobilization.	
-do-	6th		3 Officers and 97 Other Ranks proceeded on a visit to the City of LILLE.	
-do-	7th		Training carried on in the morning. 1 Officer and 50 Other Ranks proceeded on a visit to the City of LILLE. Fifteen Other Ranks proceeded to ENGLAND for demobilisation on this date.	
-do-	8th		Training carried on in vicinity of Company Billets.	
-do-	9th		A Battalion Dancing Class was formed on this date for all ranks desirous of Instruction in the Large Hall Rue St Germaine. Civilian Musicians and a piano were engaged for this purpose. Sixteen Other Ranks proceeded to ENGLAND for demobilization on 9/2/1919.	

(1).

Volume I
Sheet II

WAR DIARY of 2nd BATTALION, ROYAL IRISH RIFLES.

Army Form C. 2118.
February -1919-

Place	Date	Hour	Summary of Events and Information	Remarks and references to Appendices
			Reference Maps See p.p.1.	
MOUSCRON	10th		On this date the Battalion and Billets, Offices etc of the Unit were inspected by the Brigadier-General Commanding, 107th Infantry Brigade. 15 Other Ranks proceeded to ENGLAND for demobilization. Nominal Roll compiled of all Ranks who were selected for the Army of Occupation. On this date all Leave to U.K. was suspended except for the Army of Occupation.	
-do-	11th		Educational Classes, Dancing Classes, Lecture, etc during the morning. Fifteen Other Ranks proceeded to ENGLAND for demobilisation.	
-do-	12th		Classes etc carried on in the morning.	
-do-	13th		Classes etc during the morning. Basket Ball Match in afternoon. Twenty Other Ranks proceeded to ENGLAND for demobilisation.	
-do-	14th		Major C.W.Garner rejoined the Battalion from Leave and took over command temporarily from Captain R.O.LANSERGH who proceeded to ENGLAND, having volunteered for service in the Regular Army abroad. Ten Other Ranks proceeded to ENGLAND for demobilization.	
-do-	15th		Lieut. L.J.RICKS proceeded to the U.K. on this date for repatriation to CANADA and was struck off the strength of the Battalion. Eight Other Ranks proceeded to ENGLAND for demobilisation.	
-do-	16th		On this date Miss Lena Ashwell's Concert party gave a performance in MOUSCRON.	
-do-	17th		Educational and Recreational Training carried out during the morning. Lecture in Hall by Rev F.J.Irwin (Chaplain attached to the Unit). 8 O.R's to UK demobilised.	
-do-	18th		Five Other Ranks to ENGLAND for demobilisation.	
-do-	19th		Recreational and Educational Training carried out during the morning.	
-do-	20th		Recreational and Educational Training carried out during the morning. On this date LIEUT-COLONEL C.M.LEY BECHER, DSO rejoined the Battalion from Leave and resumed command.	
-do-	21st		Usual Training carried on. Basket Ball matches between Companies. Miss Lena Ashwell's Concert party gave a performance in the evening. On this date the personnel forming the CADRE of the Battalion was finally selected. All ranks paraded on this date who were proceeding to 12th (S) Battalion, Royal Irish Rifles.	

Volume I
Sheet III

WAR DIARY
of
~~INTELLIGENCE SUMMARY~~
2nd BATTALION ROYAL IRISH RIFLES.
(Erase heading not required.)

Army Form C. 2118.

February -1919-

Instructions regarding War Diaries and Intelligence Summaries are contained in F. S. Regs., Part II. and the Staff Manual respectively. Title pages will be prepared in manuscript.

Place	Date	Hour	Summary of Events and Information Reference Maps:- See p.p. 1.	Remarks and references to Appendices
MOUSCRON.	22nd		On this date the following Officers proceeded to join the 12th Royal Irish Rifles who were joining the Army of the Rhine:- LIEUT R.C. SCOTT M.C. LIEUT C.W. DEACON 2nd LIEUT T.R. BOND. together with 123 Other Ranks.	
-do-	23rd		Sunday - Divine Services held for all denominations. The total number of Officers and Other Ranks for transfer to 12th Battalion was 10 Officers and 189 Other Ranks. As these Officers and Other Ranks rejoined the Battalion from detachment they were sent to join the 12th Battalion.	
-do-	24th		On this date, as there were only a few details left representing the 2nd Battalion in MOUSCRON they were formed into One Company under the command of Captain W.B. TEELE. M.C. Strength of Battalion actually with the Unit was as follows:- 13 Officers 6 W.O's 13 Sergeants 4 Corporals and 64 men.	
-do-	25th		On this date 2nd LIEUT. C. RULE, 2nd LIEUT W.G. WARMER and 2nd LIEUT J.McM. WRIGHT. MC proceeded to join the 12th BN. R. Ir. Rifles.	
-do-	26th		Medical Inspection of Details carried out on this date.	
-do-	27th		On this date 12 Other Ranks from the 12th Battalion, Royal Irish Rifles joined this Unit for demobilisation purposes.	
-do-	28th		One Other Rank proceeded to ENGLAND for demobilisation.	

@@@@@@@@@@@@@@@@@@@@@@@

March 1st 1919.

C Becher
Lieut-Colonel,
Commdg; 2nd Battalion, ROYAL IRISH RIFLES.

Volume I.
Sheet I.

WAR DIARY
~~INTELLIGENCE SUMMARY~~
2nd Battalion, Royal Irish Rifles.

MARCH, 1919.

Army Form C. 2118.

Instructions regarding War Diaries and Intelligence Summaries are contained in F. S. Regs., Part II. and the Staff Manual respectively. Title pages will be prepared in manuscript.

(Erase heading not required.)

Reference Maps Sheets 28 and 29   Summary of Events and Information   Tournai 5   Dunkerque.

Place	Date	Hour	Summary of Events and Information	Remarks and references to Appendices
MOUSCRON	1st		The Battalion remained billetted in the Town of MOUSCRON, North West Flanders. 4 Other Ranks proceeded to the U.K.for demobilization.	
"	2nd		Two Other Ranks proceeded to ENGLAND for demobilization.	
"	3rd		Four Other Ranks proceeded to ENGLAND for demobilization.	
"	4th) 5th) 6th) 7th) 8th)		The Battalion remained billetted in MOUSCRON. No Other Ranks were demobilized on these dates.	
"	9th		21 Other Ranks were sent to ENGLAND on this date for demobilisation.	
"	10th		1 Other Rank demobilized.	
"	11th			
"	12th			
"	13th			
"	14th		2nd LIEUT. F. ADAMS M.C. Proceeded for duty with Chinese Labour Corps.	
"	15th			
"	16th		30 Other Ranks were sent for attachment to 15th(s) Battalion, ROYAL IRISH RIFLES, orders having been received for the Cadre of the Battalion to entrain on 17th instant for DUNKIRK.	
"	17th		Battalion entrained at MOUSCRON STATION at 12.30 hours for DUNKIRK. The following officers accompanied the Cadre :- LIEUT)COLONEL.C.M.L.BECHER D.S.O., MAJOR C.W.GARNER, CAPTAIN & ADJUTANT R.WATTS M.C., CAPTAIN W.B.TEELE M.C., LIEUT.J.REILLY M.M. The Bands of the 1st Battalion, Royal Irish Rifles and 2nd Inniskilling Fusiliers were in attendance on the Station at MOUSCRON and played during the entrainment.	
"	18th		The Train arrived at DUNKERQUE at about 02.00 hours and the Cadre detrained about 08.00 hours and proceeded to a Camp for a hot meal and a Bath, later proceeding to No.2 Camp DUNKERQUE.	

(1.)

Volume I
Sheet II

Army Form C. 2118.

Instructions regarding War Diaries and Intelligence Summaries are contained in F. S. Regs., Part II. and the Staff Manual respectively. Title pages will be prepared in manuscript.

WAR DIARY
or
INTELLIGENCE SUMMARY.
2nd Battalion, Royal Irish Rifles.

MARCH 1919.

Place	Date	Hour	Summary of Events and Information	Remarks and references to Appendices
			Ref. Maps Sheets 28 and 29. Tournai 5 Dunkerque.	
DUNKERQUE	19th		The Cadre remained at No.2 Camp, Dunkerque.	
"	20th)			
	21st)			
	22nd)			
	23rd)		The Cadre remained at No.2 Camp, Dunkerque.	
	24th)		Lieut.J.N.G.Stewart.M.C. joined the Cadre at this Camp.	
	25th)			
"	26th		The Cadre embarked at 15.05 hours on this date for SOUTHAMPTON on the Troopship "KOURSK"	

FELIXSTOWE,
30/3/1919.

Becher
Lieut-Colonel,
Commanding, 2nd Battalion, ROYAL IRISH RIFLES.

ATTACHED
36TH DIVISION
108TH INFY BDE

2ND BN ROY. IRISH RIF.
NOV - DEC 1917 - FEB 1918

Volume II. 2 Bn The Royal Irish Rifles
Sheet 1.
WAR DIARY or INTELLIGENCE SUMMARY. November 1917.
Army Form C. 2118.

Place	Date	Hour	Summary of Events and Information	Remarks and references to Appendices
In the Line	1.		Battn in Line. 2/Lt C.Rule and 2 O.R. accidentally injured. (2/Lt C.Rule and 1 O.R. remained at duty). 1 O.R. W.I.A (Self inflicted) Listening posts sent out.	
do	2		Battn in Line. Listening posts out. Our Artillery cut enemy wire opposite right Coy.	
do	3.		Battn in Line. Artillery continued wire cutting. Listening posts out at night	
do	4.		do do do. At about 9.15pm our Artillery put down a barrage in front of our line, German signals having been mistaken for our S.O.S.	
do	5		Battn in line. Listening posts out at night. Casualties 5 O.R. W.I.A.	
do	6.		do. Gas discharged from Cylinders at 10.15pm. Front line cleared except for 6 posts. Casualties from gas to R.E. Special Corps Personnel. No retaliation except a few 4.2 ins Howitzer shells in vicinity of Bn HQ and Railway. Casualties. 1 O.R. W.I.A	
do	7.		Battn in line. Trench Mortars cut enemy wire in front of left Coy. Projected gas fired from front of Brigade on left.	

WAR DIARY or INTELLIGENCE SUMMARY.

(Erase heading not required.)

Army Form C. 2118.

Place	Date	Hour	Summary of Events and Information	Remarks and references to Appendices
In the Line	8		Battn in line. Relieved by 13th Bn. The Cheshire Regt. Relief complete 3.45pm. 'D' Coy to FACTORY DUGOUTS, 'A' 'B' 'C' Coys and Bn H.Q. to ANNEQUIN. Bn H.Q. F.29.a.8.7.	
ANNEQUIN	9		Battn in Support. Working parties under 105th Field Coy R.E. 1 OR Accidentally injured.	
do	10		Battn in Support. Battn relieved in Support by the 3rd Bn. The Worcestershire Regiment (transferred from 7th to 74th Inf Bde). Relief complete 4.30pm. Battn moved by Route, (by Companies) to BETHUNE. All Coys and HQ. Unit billetted in TOBACCO FACTORY, RUE DE LILLE. Bn H.Q. 119 RUE DE LILLE.	
BETHUNE	11		Bn in BETHUNE	
do	12		do. Inspection by General HORNE, G.O.C 1st Army outside BETHUNE, at 12 noon.	
ARRAS	13		Battn embussed outside TOBACCO FACTORY at 10am, and proceeded by Bus to Third Army Area, on transfer to the 36th Division. Battn billetted in ARRAS by 2pm. Bn H.Q. 20 RUE de COCLIPAS.	

Volume II. Sheet 3.

WAR DIARY

2nd Bn The Royal Irish Rifles

Army Form C. 2118.

November 1917.

Place	Date	Hour	Summary of Events and Information	Remarks and references to Appendices
ARRAS	14		Battn embussed at 1pm on QUAI de RIVAGE, and proceeded by bus to 36th Divisional Area. Transport by March Route. Convoy travelled via BAPAUME – LE TRANSLOY – ROCQUIGNY – BUS to YTRES. Battn in Camp in LITTLE WOOD, YTRES. (Bn. H.Q.). Battn joined the 7th (Service) Bn. The Royal Irish Rifles in camp in YTRES. Major P.H. Carson, Capt C.B.J. Smyth, Capt G.A. Ogier, Capt W.A. Malone, 2/Lt W. Jones, 7th Royal Irish Rifles, Lt H.J. McConnell, 2/Lt A. Cochrane, 5th Royal Irish Rifles, Lt V.C. Young, 4th R.Ir.Rif, Lt P.A. Crawford, 2/Lt J.C. Bryans, 2/Lt F.W. Howroyd, 3rd R.Ir.Rif, Lt G.S. Roe, 2/Lt W.D. Bratby, the Royal Irish Rifles, Lt G.S. Lynch, Army Cyclist Corps, 2/Lt R.A.J. Thompson, 3rd Royal Irish Rifles, 2/Lt P.C. Kyte, 7th R.Ir.Rif, Hn.Lt & Q.M. W. Barrett, 7th R.Ir.Rif, joined the Battn on its amalgamation with the 7th (S) Bn. The Royal Irish Rifles. 515 O.R. joined the Battn from 7th R.Ir.Rif. Draft of 18 O.R. joined Battn on arrival at YTRES.	

WAR DIARY or INTELLIGENCE SUMMARY.

Army Form C. 2118.

November 1917

Place	Date	Hour	Summary of Events and Information	Remarks and references to Appendices
YTRES	15th		Battn in Camp. Reorganisation on amalgamation with 7th (S) R. Ir. Rif. Draft of 4. O.R. joined the Battn.	
YTRES	16th		Battn in Camp. Reorganisation continued. Battn paraded at 4.30 pm and proceeded by March Route to BARASTRE area. Bn in Camp (Hutments). Bn H.Q. O.10.c.9.2.	
BARASTRE	17th		Bn in Camp. Muster parade at 7.30 am. Forward area reconnoitred by Officers.	
do	18th		Bn in Camp. Training carried out. Reorganisation completed.	
do	19th		The Bn left BARASTRE at 4pm and moved to camp near LEBUCQUIERE	
LEBUCQUIERE	20th		Bn left LEBUCQUIERE 8AM and moved to some fields in vicinity of HERMIES where it remained the day in reserve during the first day of the CAMBRAI Battle. The night was spent at YORKSHIRE BANK, old British front line.	
In Field HERMIES MOEUVRES E07 3 57c	21th		Bn left Yorkshire bank and moved to Spoil HEAP. K 20 MOEUVRES E07 3 where it remained until mid-day. It then moved to the HINDENBURG LINE M K 8a 9	

WAR DIARY or INTELLIGENCE SUMMARY.

November 1917

Army Form C. 2118.

Place	Date	Hour	Summary of Events and Information	Remarks and references to Appendices
In the Field	22		At 7AM the Btn moved 1000 yards north up the HINDENBURG LINE where it remained until evening. At 7.30 pm the Btn moved up across the BAPAUME – CAMBRAI road to support the attack of the 12 RIRs on the following morning. Btn HQrs was at K2676	
In the Field MOEUVRES	23.		on the morning of the 23 the 12 RIRs attacked the village of MOEUVRES. The Battalion was in support. The 12 were held up and A B & C Coys went up in support and fought their way about ¾ of the way through the village, but had to come back owing to the fact their flanks were in the air. D Coy moved up the trench to the W of the village with the high ground as their objective, but the enemies resistance was too great. At the end of the day a line running E 20 a 46 – E 20 a 64 – E 20 b 14. Casualties. 2/Lt RAINEY. KIA. 2/Lt McALINDON WIA. OR KIA 9/6 Capt McCAREVEY WIA 2/Lt STUART. OR WIA 99 Capt SMITH WIA OR Missing 7	
In the Field	24.		The Battalion was relieved on the early morning by 11th Inniskilling Fus and marched to K13D near HERMIES. Day spent in the old British Front line	

WAR DIARY or INTELLIGENCE SUMMARY.

Army Form C. 2118.

November 1917

Place	Date	Hour	Summary of Events and Information	Remarks and references to Appendices
In the Field HERMIES	25		The Battalion remained K13D HERMIES.	
In the Field	26		At 7 pm the Battalion moved to BEAUMETZ	
BEAUMETZ	27		Battalion move to ROCQUIGNY.	
ROCQUIGNY	28			
ROCQUIGNY	29		Btn entrain at YTRES and move to SIMMONCOURT.	
GOMMICOURT	30		Btn detrained at ~~BEAUMETZ~~ ~~SIMMECOURT~~ 1.30 am and marched to The Battalion marched to GOMMICOURT where it arrived at 9 pm.	

Volume II Sheet 1

2nd Btn The Royal Irish Rifles
December 1917

WAR DIARY or INTELLIGENCE SUMMARY

Army Form C. 2118.

Vol 36

Place	Date	Hour	Summary of Events and Information	Remarks and references to Appendices
GOMIECOURT	1st		The Battalion left GOMIECOURT at 12:30 p.m. and marched to ROCQUIGNY.	
ROCQUIGNY	2nd		Btn left ROCQUIGNY at 10 A.M. and marched to fields outside METZ where it remained until 5 p.m. when it moved into Billets in METZ.	
METZ	3rd		Btn remained in METZ for the Day. At 7:30 p.m. the Btn left METZ and moved to Reserve line about Q 29 Central where it remained for the night. Draft of 3. O.R. joined Bn.	
In the Field	4th		At 6 A.M. the Btn moved north to reserve line in the vicinity of BEAUCHAMP. At 8 p.m. the Btn left this line and marched to the Trenches.	MAP. GOUZEUCOURT. E02.c Special Sheet. 20000
In the Field	5th		Btn arrived in line at 3 A.M. and relieved a Btn of the K.O.S.B. in old German line. The line held by Btn ran from L 34 d 0.8 to L 35 c 4.2. with an outpost line running L 35 c 3.2. to L 35 a 2.5. a strong point at L 35 a 2.9. from here the outpost line ran in a N.W direction held by 11/13 R. I Rifles.	

Volume II Sheet 2

WAR DIARY or INTELLIGENCE SUMMARY

December 1917

Army Form C. 2118.

Place	Date	Hour	Summary of Events and Information	Remarks and references to Appendices
In the Field	5th (cont)		The outpost line was held by B Coy, 2 pls of A Coy. 2 pl of C Coy were in a trench immediately in rear of the outpost line. The remainder of the Bttn was in the main line.	
In the Field	6th		Work was done on the outpost line which was a new trench begun by the K.O.S.B's. Enemy Patrols were very active during the night. 3 prisoners were captured during the night of whom one died. 2Lt Phillips was wounded. Draft of 4 O.R's joined.	
In the Field	7th		Inter Company relief at "Stand To" in the morning. D Coy relieved B and C Coy relieved A. 2Lt. Luck was wounded. Draft of 2 O.R's joined.	
In the Field	8th		On the night of 7/8. Bttn took over an extra piece of line from 10th R.I.F. running from L 35 c. 4.2 to R 5 a. 0.3. Line readjusted. B and C Coys holding outpost line A and D Coys in main line	

Volume II — WAR DIARY or INTELLIGENCE SUMMARY — Sheet 3 — December 1917 — Army Form C. 2118.

Place	Date	Hour	Summary of Events and Information	Remarks and references to Appendices
In the Field	9th		On night of 8/9 a Prisoner was captured by D Coy. The Commanding Officer went to F.A. Sick. Major Carson took command of the Btn. A Coy was relieved by B Coy.	
In the Field	10th		Line readjusted. 1 Coy holding the outpost line. 2 Coys holding main line. 1 Coy in reserve in Sunken road running N&S through L 34 central. This Coy was called the Counter Attack Company.	
In the Field	11th		A prisoner was captured on the night 10/11 by D Coy.	
In the Field	12th		The Battalion was relieved on the night 12/13 by the 9th R.I.F. and proceeded to Reserve line about L 32 d.	
In the Field	13th		Battalion in reserve line. At 4.30 p.m. moved up into the Support line relieving the 10th R.I.R. "A" Coy 13th attached to 107 Brigade. One Coy 11/13 Rifles attached to Battalion.	

Volume II
Sheet 4

WAR DIARY or INTELLIGENCE SUMMARY

December 1917

Army Form C. 2118.

Place	Date	Hour	Summary of Events and Information	Remarks and references to Appendices
In the Field	14th		Battalion in support line. Relieved on night 14/15 by HAWKE & NELSON Btns of the Naval Division. Btn moved to METZ for the night.	
METZ	15th		At 3pm the Btn left METZ and marched to camp at ETRICOURT.	
ETRICOURT	16th		Btn at ETRICOURT.	
ETRICOURT	17th		Btn entrained at ETRICOURT at 11 P.M. and moved to MONDICOURT by Rail. Btn marched from MONDICOURT to Billets at WARLINCOURT.	
WARLINCOURT	18th		Btn in Billets at WARLINCOURT.	
WARLINCOURT	19th		" " " " working parties clearing roads of snow.	
WARLINCOURT	20th		" " 2/Lt R.B. Marriott Watson M.C. (the Royal Irish Rifles) joined the Bn.	
WARLINCOURT	21st		" Draft of 5. O.R. joined.	
WARLINCOURT	22nd		" Draft of 18 O.R. joined.	

Volume II

WAR DIARY 2nd Bn The Royal Irish Rifles
or
INTELLIGENCE SUMMARY. December 1917

Sheet 5.

Ref Map LENS 11. 1/100,000 Amiens. Sheet 17. 1/100,000

Place	Date	Hour	Summary of Events and Information	Remarks
WARLINCOURT	23rd		Battn in billets. Training Carried out.	
do	24th		do do	
do	25th		Christmas Day. Battn in billets. Divine Services at 9.30 am.	
do	26th		Battn in billets. Renewed snowfall last night. Work recommenced on WARLINCOURT – GRINCOURT – LA BELLE VUE road. Draft of 7. O.R. joined	
do	27th		Battn in billets. Training carried out. Details of Regimental Transport proceeded by road, in advance of Bn. to Vth Army area, halting for the night at PUCHEVILLERS.	
do	28th		Battn paraded at 6.15 am and proceeded by March Route to MONDICOURT. Left there by train at 9 am. and travelled via DOULLENS, CANDAS, & AMIENS to BOVES, on transfer to 18th Corps. Fifth Army. Bn. detrained at BOVES and marched to GENTELLES arriving about 3 pm. Transport (less details which proceeded by road on 27th inst), travelled by train leaving MONDICOURT at 1 pm. This train got snowed up between CANDAS and AMIENS. (Operation order attached).	
GENTELLES	29th		Bn. in billets. Working parties all day on road between BOVES & GENTELLES	
do	30th		do. Divine Services. Working party on GENTELLES – CACHY Road. Brigadier General C.R.J. Griffith comdg 108th Inf Bde. visited the billets during the morning. Transport which proceeded by rail arrived in GENTELLES at about 2 am.	

Volume II WAR DIARY 2nd Bn. The Royal Irish Rifles Army Form C. 2118.
or
Sheet 6. INTELLIGENCE SUMMARY. December 1917.

Place	Date	Hour	Summary of Events and Information	Remarks and references to Appendices
			Ref. Map AMIENS Sheet 17 1/100,000.	
GENTELLES	31st		Battn in billets. Training carried out. Strength 36 Officers 801 OR. Trench strength 11 " " 549 "	

E. Hopkinson Major
Comdg. 2nd Bn. The Royal Irish Rifles.

Volume II 108/36 Sheet 1

WAR DIARY or INTELLIGENCE SUMMARY
(Erase heading not required.)

2nd Bn. The Royal Irish Rifles.
January 1918.

Army Form C. 2118.

Place	Date	Hour	Summary of Events and Information	Remarks and references to Appendices
GENTELLES	1st		Reference Map AMIENS Sheet 17, 1/100,000. Battn in billets. Training Continued. Working parties on GENTELLES-BOVES road, and CACHY-VILLERS BRETONNEUX road. Lt. Col. H.R. GOODMAN D.S.O. reported from Base "to England 14/12/17." Struck off Strength. 2/Lt. J.A. MORELAND accepted on probation for INDIAN Army, and struck off strength (M.S.1. India. 165963/3, dated 22/12/17).	
do	2nd		Battn in billets. Training continued.	
do	3rd		do do	
do	4th		do do. Frost continues.	
do	5th		do do. Tactical Scheme in morning. Draft of 8 O.R. joined. Lt. C.R.W. McCammond, and Lt. C.S. Roe, both previously reported as admitted to Hospital, now reported as battle casualties and struck off strength.	
do	6th		Battn in billets. Divine Services at 9.30am. Major P.H. CARSON proceeded to interview at Tank Corps H.Q. Capt. T.J.C.C. THOMPSON D.S.O. assumed temporary command of Bn. Capt. C.A. OGIER and 68 O.R. JERSEY CONTINGENT, reported to 2nd Bn. The Hampshire Regiment, 29th Division. Capt. C.A. OGIER and 60 O.R. proceeded to join 2nd Bn. The Hampshire Regt. Snow commenced at night, and rain fell. Billetting party proceeded to MARCELCAVE area.	

Volume II Sheet 2.

WAR DIARY 2nd Bn. The Royal Irish Rifles.
or
INTELLIGENCE SUMMARY.

Army Form C. 2118.

January 1918.

Reference Map AMIENS Sheet 17. 1/100,000.

Place	Date	Hour	Summary of Events and Information	Remarks and references to Appendices
GUILLAUCOURT	7th		Battn paraded in GENTELLES, and marched off at 9.45 am. Proceeded by March Route through CACHY, VILLERS BRETONNEUX, MARCELCAVE, WIENCOURT to GUILLAUCOURT. Battn in billets at GUILLAUCOURT by 2.15 pm. Thaw continued and rain fell during day. Btn HQ in CHATEAU.	
do	8th		Battn in billets. Training carried out in Morning. Lt C.R.W. McCAMMOND rejoined from Hospital. 2/Lt R.A.J. THOMPSON, R. Ir. Fus, and 2/Lt W.D. BRATBY to England, and struck off strength. Renewed snowfall and frost. Lt Col P.G.A. COX. D.S.O. 6th Bn. The Royal Dublin Fusiliers, joined the Bn and assumed command.	
do	9th		Battn in billets. Training carried out. Divisional Commander visited GUILLAUCOURT. Thaw commenced in evening.	
do	10th		Battn in billets. Continued thaw. Commanding Officer inspected all Companies. 2/Lt E.C. STROHM to hospital.	
do	11th		Battn parade at 7.10 am and proceeded by March route via HARBONNIERES, LIHONS, CHAULNES and CURCHY to NESLE area. Bn HQ in Farm 1/4 mile NW. of HERLY. 'C' and 'B' Coys billeted in HERLY. Hour of arrival 1.30 pm. 'A' and 'D' Coys billeted in BILLANCOURT.	
HERLY and BILLANCOURT	12th		Battn in billets.	
do	13th		Bn HQ, 'B' & 'C' Coys and Regtl Transport marched from HERLY at 7 am, and proceeded by March route through NESLE. 'A' and 'D' Coys joined Bn at Cross Roads 1/4 mile NE of the Y in QUIQUERRY.	

WAR DIARY or INTELLIGENCE SUMMARY.

Volume II Sheet B

2nd Bn. The Royal Irish Rifles.

Army Form C. 2118.

January 1918.

Reference Map AMIENS Sheet 17, 1/100,000. and Sheet 66 D.
ST QUENTIN Sheet 18, 1/100,000.

Place	Date	Hour	Summary of Events and Information	Remarks
HERLY	13th (cont)		Battn proceeded from this point by March route via BACQUENCOURT and HAM to ESTOUILLY and PITHON. arriving at 11.45 am. Bn HQ, billet No 19 PITHON. 'C' and 'D' Companies PITHON. 'A' and 'B' Coys in ESTOUILLY. Lieut A.M. ANDERSON rejoined Bn from Hospital, and assumed command of 'C' Coy.	
PITHON & ESTOUILLY	14th		Battn in billets. Major R. de R. ROSE M.C. rejoined the Battalion from Sick Leave	
do	15th		The Battn formed up at 10.30 am at road junction just north of the H in HAM and proceeded by March route to new billets in FLUQUIÈRES. Battn billetted in huts by 1 pm. Bn HQ. F.20.d.7.9 (Sheet 66 D). 2/Lt E.C. STRAHM rejoined from Hospital	
FLUQUIÈRES	16th		Battn in billets. Training carried out.	
do	17th		do do	
do	18th		do do. Draft of 22 O.R's joined.	
do	19th		do do. Major P. Hope CARSON accepted for service with TANK Corps, and struck off strength (Auty A.G/114/61(O) dated 12/1/18).	
do	20th		Battn in billets. Reorganisation of Companies, forming 4 four platoons.	
do	21st		do Training under Platoon Commanders. 2/Lt P.A.I. CRAWFORD reported to U.K and struck off Strength	

Volume II. Sheet 4.

WAR DIARY 2nd Bn. The Royal Irish Rifles
or
INTELLIGENCE SUMMARY.
January 1918.
Army Form C. 2118.

Reference Maps ST. QUENTIN Sheet 18, 1/100,000. & Sheet 66D 1/40,000.

Place	Date	Hour	Summary of Events and Information	Remarks and references to Appendices
FLUQUIÈRES	22nd		Battn in billets. Inspection by Divisional Commander (Maj Gen O.S.W.NUGENT ADC, DSO.) at 11 am at F.20.a central. Battn in Full Marching Order.	
do	23rd		Battn in billets. Training carried out. Conference at Bde H.Q. with reference to work on defences.	
do	24th		Battn in billets. Training continued.	
do	25th		Battn in billets. All Companies at work on defences of battle zone. Line of trenches started. E. of ROUPY.	
do	26th		Battn in billets. Work continued. Lt Col P.G.A.COX DSO assumed temporary command of 108th Inf. Bde., during absence on leave of Brigadier Gen. C.R.J. GRIFFITH CMG DSO. Major R. de R. Rose MC assumed temporary command of the Battn.	
do	27th		Battn in billets. A & B. Coys working. C and D Coys marched to ARTEMPS for distribution of Medal Ribbons by Divisional Commander. Maj H.W. FOSTER M.C. and 2nd Lt M.A. McFERRAN M.C. received M.C. ribbons. 2/Lt W.L.P. DOBBIN M.C. returned from 14th Inf. Bde. H.Q. 2/Lt LT RICKS returned from Hospital	
do	28th		Battn in billets. Battn paraded at 3.30 pm and proceeded	

Volume II — WAR DIARY or INTELLIGENCE SUMMARY — 2nd Bn. The Royal Irish Rifles — Army Form C. 2118.

Sheet 5. — January 1918.

Place	Date	Hour	Summary of Events and Information	Remarks and references to Appendices
			Reference Maps 66D and 66C. N.W.	
FLUQUIERES	28		by March Route via HAPPENCOURT and GRAND SERAUCOURT to Railway Cutting G.6.c., relieving 10th Bn. The Royal Inniskilling Fusiliers in Bde Reserve (Right Sector, 36th Divisional Front). Relief complete at 7.30 am. Battn in Dug outs along Railway Cutting. Bn. HQ. G.6.a.6.4.	
In the Field	29.		Battn in Dug outs. Officers reconnoitring line in the morning. Battn paraded in Railway Cutting at 6 pm and proceeded by March Route via ESSIGNY to the line, by Platoons at 100 yds distance. Battn relieved the 11th (S) Bn. The Royal Inniskilling Fusiliers in line between G.1.b.4.0 and G.9.b.10.4. Relief Complete at 10 pm. Battn HQ. G.14.a.5.0. Quiet night. 'C' Coy right front line, 'D' Coy left front line, 'A' Coy Counter Attack position, 'B' Coy Passive Defence.	
In the Line	30.		Battn in the Line. Very quiet. Work and Wiring carried out.	
do	31.		do do do.	

Fighting Strength 29 Officers 773 O.R's
Trench " 16 " 423 "

R W Rose Major
Commanding 2nd Bn The Royal Irish Rifles

Volume II — **WAR DIARY** 2nd Bn The Royal Irish Rifles — Army Form C. 2118.
Sheet 1. or **INTELLIGENCE SUMMARY.** February 1918

Reference Map. Sheet 66 C. NW 1/20,000

Place	Date	Hour	Summary of Events and Information	Remarks and references to Appendices
In the Line	1.		Battn in the line. Patrol sent out at night. 1 O.R. W.I.A.	
do	2		do. Wiring carried out. 1 O.R. W.I.A.	
do	3		Battn in the line. Capt PATRICK WILLIAM KEATING, The Royal Irish Rifles, joined the Battn. Patrol sent out at night.	
do	4th		Battn in line. Enemy Artillery slightly more active. Battn relieved by the 11/13th Royal Irish Rifles. Relief Complete 9.30 p.m. On relief Platoons moved into Brigade Reserve at ESSIGNY STATION. C.6.C. Instructions received regarding reorganisation of the Army.	
C.6.a.& c.	5th		Battn in Dug outs. C and D Coys working in forward area during the evening.	
do	6th		Battn in Dug outs. Capt & Adjutant C.F. WILKINS D.S.O. M.C. rejoined from First Army Headquarters. Lieut JOHN KEMMY BOYLE M.C. 7th Bn. The Royal Dublin Fusiliers joined the Battn. A & B Coys continued work begun on previous night.	
do	7th		Battn in Dug outs. Lieut RICHARD FERRAR PATTERSON, 9th Bn The Royal Irish Rifles, Lieut THOMAS HASTINGS WITHEROW, 8th Bn. The Royal Irish Rifles, and 123 O.R (late 8/9th R.I. Rif) joined the Battn on disbandment of the 8/9th (Service) Bn. The Royal Irish Rifles. C and D Coys continued work at night.	

Volume II
Sheet 2

2nd Bn. The Royal Irish Rifles

WAR DIARY
or
INTELLIGENCE SUMMARY.
(Erase heading not required.)

Army Form C. 2118.

February 1918.

Reference Maps ST QUENTIN Sheet 13, 1/100,000, Sheets 66 D and 66 C and 62 B.

Place	Date	Hour	Summary of Events and Information	Remarks and references to Appendices
In Dugouts	8	5.30 p.m.	The Battalion was transferred from the 108th to 107th Brigade. Bn. left dugouts in G.6.a.x.c. and moved into Reserve Area of 107th Brigade in A.9.a. Taking over from the 1st Royal Irish Fusiliers	
	9		Battalion proceeded to line in the evening, the first Coy marching off at 5.30 p.m. and relieved the 10th Royal Irish Rifles. C & D Coys in the front line. A Coy Counter attack Coy. and B Coy Passive Resistance Coy. The line held by the Battalion extended from S.23.c.8.0.70 — to Canal inclu. Battalion HQ at S.28.b.20.20	
In the Line	10		Battalion in the line. Patrol consisting of 2 Offrs and 20 ORs sent out. Bn HQ move to A.30.d.70.30	
	11		Battalion in the line. Patrol consisting of 1 Off & 20 OR.	
	12		Battalion in line Patrol 1 Off & 20 other Rks.	
	13		" "	
	14		" 1 OR. W. + A.	

Volume II 2nd Bn the Royal Irish Rifles

WAR DIARY
or
INTELLIGENCE SUMMARY.

Sheet 2

February 1918

Army Form C. 2118.

Ref map Sheet 62 B.S.W. + 66 C. N.W.

Place	Date	Hour	Summary of Events and Information	Remarks and references to Appendices
Antheline	15		Battalion in line. Battalion relieved by the 1st Bn Inniskillen Fusiliers. Relief complete 11 p.m. Battalion move by Companies independently to FLUQUIERES.	
FLUQUIERES	16		Battalion in Billets. draft consisting of 3 off 48 O.R.s joined. 2/Lieut H. Marshall, 2/Lieut D. Leslie, 2/Lieut R. Gough	
"	17		Battn in Billets. Working parties furnished	
	18		— do —	
	19		— do —	
	20		— do —	
Gd SERAUCOURT	21		Battn moved by Route to Gd SERACOURT. Capt G.E. LINDSAY R.A.M.C. joined relieving Capt C.C.G. GIBSON to 109th F.A.	
	22		Battn in Billets Gd SERACOURT. Working parties furnished 3 O.R. to 2nd HANTS. Regt.	
	23		Battn in billets. Working parties furnished	

Volume II — WAR DIARY or INTELLIGENCE SUMMARY — 2nd Bn. The Roy. Ir. Rifles — Army Form C. 2118.
Sheet 3 — February 1918

66c N.W.

Place	Date	Hour	Summary of Events and Information	Remarks and references to Appendices
Gd SERAUCOURT	24		Battn in billets. Working parties furnished. Draft Capt W A MALONE (2) Bn the Royal Irish Rifles + 56 O.R. joined	
	25		Battn in billets - working parties furnished	
	26		— do —	
	27		— do —	
	28		— do — Battn moved into Support and are located at QUARRIES. G 3 a & B. and A 27 c.	

Strength   O   OR.
Trench   18   551
Fighting   20   684
Total   41   967

R.d.P. Rose Major.
Commdg. Roy. Ir. Rifles.

www.ingramcontent.com/pod-product-compliance
Lightning Source LLC
Chambersburg PA
CBHW081239170426
43191CB00034B/1979